SWEET-VOICED SAPPHO

THE POETIC WORK OF THEODORE STEPHANIDES

This is the first volume in the projected publication or republication by Colenso Books of all the original poetry, verse drama and poetic translations of Theodore Stephanides, including the translations made in co-operation with George Katsimbalis.

ORIGINAL POETRY AND DRAMA BY STEPHANIDES
The Collected Poems of Theodore Stephanides
including the four published collections: *The Golden Face
Cities of the Mind — Worlds in a Crucible — Autumn Gleanings*
(of which only the last is in print) and a few additional poems
The Complete Plays of Theodore Stephanides
(*The Bridge of Arta — Labyrinth — Arodaphnousa
Karaghiozis, Alexander the Great, and the Dreadful Dragon
Karaghiozis and the Enchanted Tree*)

TRANSLATIONS BY STEPHANIDES ALONE
Sweet-voiced Sappho (2015)
Erotocritos by VITZENTZOS KORNAROS
Life and Death in Modern Greek Folk Poetry

TRANSLATIONS BY STEPHANIDES AND KATSIMBALIS
Modern Greek Poetry: An Anthology
*Life Immutable, The King's Flute, The Twelve
Words of the Gypsy, and Other Poems*
by KOSTIS PALAMAS

OTHER WORKS OF GREEK LITERATURE FROM COLENSO BOOKS
Three Plays by IAKOVOS KAMBANELLIS
(*The Courtyard of Wonders —The Four Legs of the Table — Ibsenland*)
translated by Marjorie Chambers, 2015
The Life and Death of Hangman Thomas — Corfiot Tales
by KONSTANTINOS THEOTOKIS
translated by J. M. Q. Davies (expected 2015 and 2016)

Sweet-voiced Sappho

SOME OF THE EXTANT POEMS
OF SAPPHO OF LESBOS

AND

OTHER ANCIENT GREEK POEMS

translated by

Theodore Stephanides

edited by Anthony Hirst

with facing Greek text

COLENSO BOOKS
2015

First published by Colenso Books 2015

Colenso Books
68 Palatine Road, London N16 8ST, UK
colensobooks@gmail.com
Reprinted with minor corrections February 2016

ISBN 978-0-9928632-3-4

Translations Copyright © 2015 the Estate of Theodore Stephanides

Introduction and Notes Copyright © 2015 Anthony Hirst

Sixteen lines of Greek text from page 34 of *Sappho and Alcaeus: An Introduction to the Study of Ancient Lesbian Poetry* by Denys Page (1955) are reproduced (on page 28) by permission of Oxford University Press.

The remainder of the Greek text is from editions now in the public domain.

The font used for the Greek text is GraecaUBS by Linguists Software (P.O. Box 580, Edmonds, WA, 98020 USA – info@linguistsoftware.com). The rest of the book is set in Garamond, with Helvetica for some headings.

The image on the front cover is a Roman head of Sappho in the Archaeological Museum in Istanbul. It is based on a lost Hellenistic original, and was found at Izmir (Smyrna). The photograph is by Richard Hellinga and is reproduced with his permission.

Printed and bound in Great Britain by
Lightning Source UK Ltd
Chapter House, Pitfield, Kiln Farm,
Milton Keynes MK11 3LW, UK

CONTENTS

Introduction	vii
The Tenth Muse by Theodore Stephanides	1
Sappho: Distichs	3
Love – The doves – The river – The lyre – The song – Death	5
To the Muses – Invocation – The girdle – Night prayer – Night – Moonrise	7
Morning – Flowers – Prayer – Dying Sappho to her daughter Cleis	9
Sappho: Quatrains and other short poems	11
Retrospect – The boor – Wealth and Virtue – Gold	13
To her baby daughter Cleis – Epitaph – Wine – To Dica	15
Complaint – Love-sickness – The apple – The altar	17
The garden – Bluebells – The cicada – Evening	19
Moonlight – Alcaeus and Sappho – To Atthis	21
To a friend – The return – Gorgo	23
Longer poems of Sappho	25
After the marriage ceremony – The farewell	27
To Aphrodite of Knossos	29
Sappho's lament to Aphrodite	31
To a dream	33
Love	35
The departure of Anactoria	37
To Anactoria	39
Farewell to Atthis	41

CONTENTS

On Gongyla's departure	43
Sappho to her pupils	45
Sappho greets her pupils	47
Sappho refuses to marry again	49
Sappho in exile	51
Dying Sappho to Gongyla	53
Setting Pleiades by Theodore Stephanides	55
Short poems of other Ancient Greek authors	57
Life (Palladas)	59
Sepulchral epigram (Plato)	59
Lais' mirror (Plato)	59
The Tenth Muse (Plato)	61
Appearance (Epictetus)	61
The astronomer (Claudius Ptolemaeus)	61
The lover (Anacreon)	63
The exile (Julius Polyaenus)	63
Epitaph for Leonidas and his Three Hundred (Simonides)	63
Epitaph to the Spartan dead at Plataea (Simonides)	65
Epitaph to a Maltese watch-dog (Tymnes)	65
The hypochondriac's epitaph (Anon.)	65
Notes on the poems of Sappho	67
Notes on the poems of other Ancient Greek authors	75
Sources of the Greek texts and translations	79
Index of persons and places	82
Greek index of first lines	84
English index of titles and first lines	86

INTRODUCTION

This is the first of a projected series of volumes intended to include all of the translations of Greek poetry by Theodore Stephanides (1896–1983), ranging from Sappho to the twentieth century and including those translations made in conjunction with George Katsimbalis (1899–1978).

With very few exceptions, these verse translations of Sappho and other Ancient Greek authors are published here for the first time. Most are to be found in a bound carbon-copy typescript (referred to below as "the *Typescript*") which Theodore Stephanides deposited in the British Library, most probably in 1978, since the title page bears the hand-written inscription, "With the translator's best wishes Th. Stephanides London, June 1978".

The *Typescript* has the title "Translations of some of the extant poems of Sappho of Lesbos (*circa* 620 B.C.)", but it also contains nine translations from other poets of Ancient Greece, and two lines from Alcaeus that accompany one of the Sappho translations to form the dialogue "Alcaeus and Sappho".

The title of this volume, *Sweet-voiced Sappho*, was not provided by Stephanides, but in part derives from Sappho herself, since the adjective (*aduphônos*) meaning precisely "sweet-voiced" occurs in a two-word fragment of her poetry: just the phrase *parthenon aduphônon* ("sweet-voiced girl").[1] In "Sappho to her pupils", Stephanides has the pupils say "We'll crown Sappho for her *sweet voice* today". This is, however, a rather free translation, and it is actually the sweetness of her lyre that the Greek refers to: "player of the clear sweet lyre" in Edmonds' translation. Nonetheless, Stephanides' free translation helps justify the present title. And, besides, Antipater of Sidon refers to the works "of honey-voiced Sappho" (*meliphônou Sapphous*).[2]

The subtitle includes a modified from of the title of the

---

[1] *Lyra Graeca* I, Sappho 102.
[2] *Greek Anthology* III, Book IX, 66.

INTRODUCTION

Typescript, from which the date "*circa* 620 B.C." has been removed. It is not clear what this date was meant to refer to, but 620 BC is within the date range usually suggested for Sappho's birth and is almost certainly too early for any of her poetry.

This small volume is divided into four sections, the first three for Sappho's poems, grouped by length; the fourth for poems of other Ancient Greek authors. The heading of the first Sappho section, "Distichs", is taken from the Contents page at the back of the *Typescript* rather than from the text, although there is also a footnote in the *Typescript*, on the first page of distichs, which reads "Most of these distichs are probably fragments of longer poems". The only other heading among the poems of Sappho in Stephanides' Contents is "Longer Poems". This is placed after "Dying Sappho to her daughter Cleis", the last of Stephanides' distichs, and before "Retrospect", which is the first of twenty-one poems of three-to-six lines, of which eighteen consist of four lines. The last of these twenty-one poems is "The return" (five lines). All the poems of Sappho following "The return" are of eight or more lines. I have, therefore, introduced an intermediate heading "Quatrains and other short poems", for the first of these groups, and reserved "Longer poems" for those poems of eight or more lines (the longest has twenty-eight lines) which begin with "After the marriage ceremony". "Quatrains" is a term used frequently in Stephanides' volumes of his own English poetry, where small groups of such poems are presented together on a page with headings such as "Four quatrains"; and in fact Sappho's "The Altar" and "Complaint" (the latter with the title "Lament") appear as the first two of "Four Quatrains" on page 29 of *Worlds in a Crucible*, the third of Stephanides' four collections of original English poetry.

In the *Typescript*'s Contents the nine poems by poets other than Sappho are simply headed "Other Translations". I have replaced this by the more informative heading "Short poems of other Ancient Greek authors".

The *Typescript* includes Stephanides' own poem on Sappho,

viii

INTRODUCTION

"The Tenth Muse" (from *Worlds in a Crucible*), placed at the end, as an "Addendum". I have preferred to put this before the translations, as a kind of prologue, and have added, after the last of the Sappho translations, Stephanides' other original poem which refers to Sappho, "Setting Pleiades" (from *Cities of the Mind*), to serve as an afterword.

Stephanides' poem "The Tenth Muse" incorporates translations of three fragments of Sappho, and an epigram attributed to Plato which names Sappho the Tenth Muse. Diffcrent versions of two of these Sappho fragments appear in the *Typescript*, and I have added the third, "Gorgo" — that line which might be "all that *will* survive" of Sappho's work in the distant future — placing it at the end of the Quatrains section.

To the nine poems by other Greek authors in the final section I have added Plato's epigram on Sappho as the Tenth Muse, along with two other translations from Ancient Greek found in Stephanides' published works: Simonides' "Epitaph for Leonidas and his Three Hundred" from *Island Trails* and "The hypochondriac's epitaph" from *Autumn Gleanings*. The first two accompany other poems by their respective authors; the humorous and anonymous epitaph is placed at the end.

The titles of the individual poems are, in most cases, provided by Stephanides rather than taken from the sources. Where the Greek sources do include titles for the poems or fragments of Sappho, these are all in the same format, simply defining the person (or, in once case, impersonal entity) addressed: "To Timas", "To Hera" or "To a dream", and so on. Stephanides adopts only a few of these. Had he adopted all the sixteen titles available, he would have had two poems entitled "To Aphrodite" and two entitled "To Atthis".

I have modified two of Stephanides' titles because they seemed to embody a misconception on his part. There are two poems which concern Gongyla, one of Sappho's lovers, or companions, or "pupils": "On Gongyla's departure" and "Dying Sappho to Gongyla". Stephanides seems to have believed that

INTRODUCTION

Gongyla was Sappho's daugher, since, in the *Typescript* these poems are entitled "On her daughter's departure from home" and "Dying Sappho to her daughter Gongyla". It is generally accepted that Sappho had one daughter, Kleïs, named after her mother. The daughter's name, in the form "Cleis", figures in a further two of Stephanides' titles: "Dying Sappho to her daughter Cleis" and "To her baby daughter Cleis"; and the poem to which the second of these titles is attached does indeed refer to Cleis by name. While it has sometimes been argued that Cleis was a companion rather than a daughter of Sappho, no one other than Stephanides has, as far as I can determine, ever suggested that Sappho had two daughters or that Gongyla was her daughter. Hence my removal of the word "daughter" from the two titles concerned.

Another problematic title is "To Anactoria", attached, in the *Typescript*, to the poem beginning "Beyond all other mortals is he blessed". Although Anactoria figures in the next two poems in Stephanides' sequence, "On the departure of Anactoria" and the poem which begins "Some claim the fairest thing on this dark earth", and which is entitled "Love" in the *Typescript*, she is not mentioned at all in the poem that Stephanides calls "To Anactoria". And, what is more, the Greek text is addressed to someone by another name, Brocheo or Brochea (it appears in the abbreviated form *Broche'* in stanza 2, line 3), but this name does not appear in the translation. If, as Edmonds suggests, *Broche'* is derived from *brachus* meaning "short" it may well be a nickname, but there is nothing to suggest its association with Anactoria. Furthermore, in Edmonds' editions of *Lyra Graeca* (and in other editions of Sappho) it is the poem beginning "Some claim the fairest thing on this dark earth" that has the title "To Anactoria", which is found in Greek (*pros Anaktorian*) in the papyrus fragment from Oxyrhynchus which is the ultimate source of the poem. This suggests a simple solution to the problem of Stephanides' titles, namely, that they got mixed up in the production of the *Typescript*, and that "To Anactoria" should have been applied to the poem which has this title in Greek, and

INTRODUCTION

"Love" to the poem which, in Greek, is untitled and addressed to Brocheo, and so I have switched these two titles around.

While it is not intended that all subsequent volumes of Stephanides' poetic translations in this series will be dual-language, I felt that in the case of the Sappho translations it was essential to identify and include the Greek texts which Stephanides had translated, given that among the many editions of the Greek texts of Sappho there is wide variation in the way the mostly fragmentary poems are restored (or not), and no universally accepted sequence or numbering system that one can refer to. And, as Peter Green noted recently, because of the wide variation in the extent and content of the restoration of the text by different editors, the publication of translations of Sappho is "a case crying out for a double-page presentation of English and Greek, the latter consisting, at the minimum, of the editor's text from which the translator worked".[3]

Though with less need in most cases, Greek texts are also provided for Stephanides' translations from other Ancient Greek authors.

Where Sappho is concerned, the Greek texts on the left-hand pages, facing the translations, may not be the latest or most reliable versions of the fragments of her poems, and do not benefit from the more recent fruits of scholarship, since they are taken, for the most part, from an early volume in the Loeb series, published in the third decade of the twentieth century.

It has not been possible to determine with absolute certainty which editions of the Greek texts Stephanides used, but there is a very strong probability that for Sappho his principal source was the first edition of *Lyra Graeca* volume I, edited by J. M. Edmonds and published, in the Loeb series, in 1922. Edmonds' "second and enlarged edition" of 1928 differs at many points in

---

[3] Peter Green, "What we know", a review of *Sappho: A New Translation of the Complete Works*, by Diane Raynor. *London Review of Books*, 19 November 2015, page 21.

INTRODUCTION

its reconstruction of the texts; it also provides, in an Appendix, some extra poems by Sappho and other authors. Three of the additional Sappho poems appear in the present volume and the 1928 edition of *Lyra Graeca* may well have been Stephanides' source for these. It is easy to show, though, that if he used Edmonds' Greek texts for the other poems it was the first edition of 1922 that he used. Two examples will suffice.

"Dying Sappho to Gongyla" ends — and here Sappho is quoting herself addressing the god Hermes — "you guided Agamemnon and the flower / of the Achaeans in their past renown". Edmonds' 1922 edition contains at this point the partially restored abbreviated word *Agamemnon'*, but in his 1928 edition this is quite differently restored as *Acherontos* (the river Acheron) and all subsequent words of his earlier Greek text, with their clear reference to the "flower of the Achaeans" (*anthos Achaiiôn*), are omitted.

The second example is "Farewell to Atthis", where Edmonds' 1928 edition is two-and-a-half stanzas longer than that of 1922. Stephanides' translation stops at the same point as Edmonds' earlier version, whose final phrase is *potôn glukiôn*, from which Stephanides gets his closing phrase "spicèd wine" (but literally "sweet drinks"). In Edmonds' later restoration this phrase appears as *abron Ianidôn*, which has nothing to do with drink but refers to a "delicate-living Ionian", in Edmonds' own translation. This may be a more plausible restoration, but it is clearly not what Stephanides had in front of him.

One of the longer poems of Sappho which Stephanides translates, "To Aphrodite of Knossos", was known only as a short fragment of three-and-a-half lines[4] until 1937, when a much longer though still incomplete version discovered on a potsherd was first published. For this poem I have provided the Greek text from Denys Page's *Sappho and Alcaeus*. Page's text is, like those of Edmonds, highly if not quite fully restored. Then for "Prayer" I have had recourse to an edition older than

---

[4] See *Lyra Graeca* I, Sappho 4.

Edmonds', namely Wharton's *Sappho*, since the fragment published by Edmonds consists of only the first three of the ten words of Wharton's Greek text.[5] Wharton has also been used for "Retrospect". In this case the two lines of Wharton's Greek text do occur in Edmonds, but as part of a longer poem "Sappho to her pupils", which Stephanides has also translated — probably at a later date (for further information see the Notes).

It is clear that Stephanides must have been translating from highly restored versions of Sappho's Greek, as one small, if extreme, example will illustrate. For the fourth stanza of "Sappho in exile", a poem addressed to the goddess Hera, Stephanides has:

>Let me return to Mytilene's fields
>among the maidens whom, in other days,
>I taught to dance before your holy shrine
>and sing your joyous praise.

This matches fairly closely Edmonds' heavily restored Greek text, as can be seen from his more-or-less literal translation that accompanies it: "that ... I may do again, as of old, things pure and beautiful among the maids of Mytilene, whom I have so often taught to dance and sing upon thy feast days". But compare this with Anne Carson's version in *If not, winter* (page 31). Translating only what is actually preserved and can be construed beyond any doubt, she has for this stanza just five words:

>Holy and beautiful
>maiden
>around[
>   ]

Restorations such as those in *Lyra Graeca* are to a considerable extent speculative, resulting in plausible but highly uncertain recreations of Sappho's verse. Stephanides' translations of such speculative recreations are often rather free, and thus they stand at two removes — but two creative and

---

[5] See *Lyra Graeca* I, Sappho 17.

imaginative removes — from the elusive texts of Sappho. Nevertheless, in their simplicity and immediacy, they may give us more of a sense of Sappho's voice than a scrupulously accurate prose rendering of disconnected words and phrases.

Nine of the twelve poems in the final section, "Short poems of other Ancient Greek authors", can be found in the *The Greek Anthology*, a medieval compendium of Greek verse (mainly epigrams), based on three much earlier anthologies, with contents dating from the seventh century BC to around AD 1000. In the *Typescript*, though, it is only in relation to the "Epitaph to a Maltese watch-dog" that Stephanides makes any reference to the *Anthology*. For these nine, I have used the texts from the first Loeb edition of *The Greek Anthology* (1915–1918), though the two sepulchral epigrams by Simonides are also in *Lyra Graeca* II. The source of the quatrain entitled "Appearance", which Stephanides designates as "After Epictetus", is not to be found in *The Greek Anthology* since Epictetus (a Stoic philosopher) did not write poetry. For this I have provided a brief extract from Schenkl's edition of Epictetus for the first two lines of the quatrain (the third and fourth lines seem not to have a specific source). The other two poems not found in the *Anthology* are "The lover" by Anacreon and "The hypochodriac's epitaph". The former is in *Lyra Graeca* II, but for the latter no source has yet been traced.

Each Greek text is followed by a source reference, while the source of a translation is only given where it is not from the *Typescript* in the British Library (e.g. "*Island Trails,* page 18" for Simonides' "Epitaph for Leonidas..."), or where it is in the *Typescript* but also in one of Stephanides' published works (e.g. "*Typescript* and *Worlds in a Crucible,* page 29" for Sappho's "The Altar"). Source references for the Greek texts consist of a short form of the title (sometimes with the editor's name in brackets), followed either by the name of the Greek author and the number of the poem of that author (in the case of poems in *Lyra Graeca*), or by the number of the Book and number of the poem within the Book in the case of poems from *The Greek Anthology*.

The short titles of all the sources cited (for both Greek texts and translations) will be found in the list of Sources on pages 79–81, each followed by full publication details.

Where the poems and fragments of Sappho are concerned, the Greek texts do not usually appear exactly as found in the sources. The frequent square brackets surrounding those parts of the text which are editorial restoration have been omitted, as have the dots below individual letters considered uncertain, as well as the curved lines below the text joining groups of vowels to be treated as belonging to a single syllable for metrical purposes. These restored Greek texts, as noted above, are creative constructs, and in this volume, where their only function is to provide a Greek version of each poem corresponding as closely as possible to Stephanides' translation, it would serve no purpose to reproduce the scholarly marks of restoration. Rows of spaced stops, indicating gaps in the text where restoration has not been attempted are, however, retained. Where a word or phrase in *Lyra Graeca* I is without diacritic marks (and without explanation for their absence) these have been added on the basis of *Lyra Greaca* Ia or other authorities.

Those who know Ancient Greek but are not familiar with the Aeolic dialect will find many strange things in the Greek texts of Sappho. These include double consonants where single consonants would be expected, recessive accentuation, and the substitution of *alpha* for *eta*. Aeolic σέλαννα for Attic σελήνη (meaning "moon"), illustrates all three of these features. Then there is the very frequent ἀπὺ and ἀπυ- for ἀπὸ and ἀπο- (among many differences in spelling), the absence of rough breathings (aspiration being largely absent from Aeolic), and several occurences of *vau* or *digamma* (ϝ), equivalent to the English letter *w*. The *digamma* was not restricted to Aeolic, but was a feature of many early Greek texts, and was retained in Aeolic and Doric long after it disappeared from Attic and Ionic. The *digamma* often needs to be restored to early poetic texts (including Homer) to resolve apparent metrical defects.

INTRODUCTION

At the end of the book will be found Notes to the poems. These deal with such things as the relationship between the translations and the Greek texts, differences between versions of the translations, and thematic links between certain poems. They also provide information about people and places from Greek mythology and history to which the poems refer or allude (assuming only that Zeus, Aphrodite, Eros, the Muses and Troy need no explanation). The notes follow the order of the poems in the book, and each one begins with the title of the poem, preceded by the number of the page on which the translation is found.

The Notes are followed by the list of Sources already mentioned; and finally there are three indexes: an index of persons and places referred to, a Greek index of first lines and an English index of titles and first lines.

The sources from which I have taken the Greek texts are, with one exception, in the public domain. I am grateful to Harvard University Press for confirming this where the Loeb editions are concerned. The Greek text of Sappho's "To Aphrodite of Knossos" is reproduced by permission of Oxford University Press from Denys Page's *Sappho and Alcaeus*. I am grateful to Richard Hellinga for permission to use his photograph of a portrait head of Sappho on the front cover, and to Natasha Fagelman, Ahuvia Kahane, and Michael Silk for suggestions that have helped in tracing some of the more elusive sources. I am greatly indebted to my friend and colleague Paddy Sammon for proof-reading the entire book three times, thus saving me from many errors, for providing text for the back cover, and for suggesting several useful additions to the Introduction and Notes. Finally, but above all, I thank Alexia Stephanides Mercouri for her friendship and encouragement, and her enthusiasm for the publication or republication of her father's work.

Anthony Hirst.
London, November 2015

The Tenth Muse

Such was the reverence and awe inspired
by Sappho's verse in ancient Grecian times,
that Plato even could declare: "Some say
there are Nine Muses — let them think again,
for Lesbian Sappho should be hailed the Tenth!"

Such was her bygone fame. Yet in our day
nothing remains of Sappho's poetry
except a mere six hundred lines or so;
some matchless in their beauty, some too tattered,
fragmented, garbled, patched, to be of worth.
Among the former is that yearning plaint:
The moon has set, the Pleiades are sinking
out of the sky. The hour is late. The night
is almost past . . . yet here I lie, alone.
Or else that happier picture of a garden:
There is the song of water all around
through channel troughs of apple-wood; and sleep
drifts down on me from the cool, rustling leaves.
But, with these lines, others have been preserved
to reach us, out of context, from the past;
lines such as: *Gorgo . . . I am sick of her!*

How sad it would have been if, by some jest
of ribald, mocking Fate, that single line
had been the only one to bridge the years
of all the songs of Sappho, the Tenth Muse!

But here Fate grins and chuckles: "Man is mad,
his passion for destruction limitless.
Perhaps in twenty-six more centuries,
that line alone is all that *will* survive!"

Theodore Stephanides
Typescript and *Worlds in a Crucible*, page 28

SAPPHO

DISTICHS

Most of these distichs are probably
fragments of longer poems.

*It is Stephanides' translations which are
all distichs (or, more precisely, rhyming couplets);
the Greek poetic fragments of Sappho in this
section vary from one to three lines in length.*

Love

ἔμοι δ' ὡς ἄνεμος κατάρης δρύσιν ἐμπέτων
ἐτίναξεν ἔρος φρένας . . . . . .

Lyra Graeca I, Sappho 54

The doves

ταῖσι δὲ ψαῦκρος μὲν ἔγεντο θῦμος
πὰρ δ' ἴεισι τὰ πτέρα . . .

Lyra Graeca I, Sappho 16

The river

χρύσειοι δ' ἐρέβινθοι ἐπ' ἀϊόνων ἐφύοντο.

Lyra Graeca I, Sappho 139

The lyre

Ἄγε δῖα χέλυννά μοι
φωνάεσσά τε γίγνεο·

Lyra Graeca I, Sappho 80

The song

. . . τάδε νῦν ἑταίραις
ταῖς ἔμαισι τέρπνα κάλως ἀείσω.

Lyra Graeca I, Sappho 12

Death

τὸ θναίσκην κάκον· οἱ θέοι γὰρ οὕτω
κεκρίκαισι· θάνον κε γάρ.

Lyra Graeca I, Sappho 91

DISTICHS

Love
The oak-tree bends before the headlong wind,
and thus does Love assail and shake my mind!

The doves
Ah, see the love-sick doves, poor things;
see, when rebuffed, how they do droop their wings . . .

The river
The river flows, cold from the mountain snow,
and on its banks the golden vetches grow.

The lyre
O come, my lyre divine, take wing;
make of yourself a singing thing.

The song
A song I will now sing and, at my voice,
all who are awed by beauty shall rejoice.

Death
Death is an evil — thus the gods decide.
Were it not so, they would themselves have died.

To the Muses
ἀλλ' ἔμ' ὀλβίαν ἀδόλως ἔθηκαν
χρύσιαι Μοῖσαι οὐδ' ἔμεθεν θανοίσας
ἔσσεται λάθα. . . . .
Lyra Graeca I, Sappho 11

Invocation
Δεῦρο δηὖτε, Μοῖσαι, χρύσιον λίποισαι
δῶμα . . . .
Lyra Graeca I, Sappho 129

The girdle
. . . . πόδας δὲ
ποίκιλος μάσλης ἐπέτεννε, Λύδι-
ον κάλον ἔργον.
Lyra Graeca I, Sappho 20

Night prayer
. . . . . τοῦτο δ' ἴσθι, διπλασίαν
κῆναν νύκτ' ἄρασθαί μ' ἄμμι γένεσθαι.
Lyra Graeca I, Sappho 84A

Night
ψαύην δ' οὐ δοκίμοιμ' ὀράνω ἔσσα διπάχεα.
Lyra Graeca I, Sappho 53

Moonrise
πλήρης μὲν ἐφαίνετ' ἀ σέλαννα,
αἰ δ' ὡς περὶ βῶμον ἐστάθησαν . . .
Lyra Graeca I, Sappho 112

To the Muses
The Golden Muses gave me all delight;
nor shall I be forgotten in death's night . . .

Invocation
Your golden home, O Muses, on this day
abandon for a while and come my way.

The girdle
Her girdle's fringe hung to her ankles down,
fair workmanship from some far Lydian town.

Night prayer
Through these sweet hours, believe me when I say
I prayed our night would halt intruding day.

Night
I did not ever guess, until one night I tried,
that my arms could embrace the stars of eventide.

Moonrise
Full gleams the moon; and young girls gaze
around an altar's sacred blaze.

Morning
. . . . . . ἀλλ' ἄγιτ', ὦ φίλαι,
ἀοίδας ἀπυλήξομεν, ἄγχι γὰρ ἀμέρα.
Lyra Graeca I, Sappho 65

Flowers
Ποικίλλεται μὲν γαῖα πολυστέφανος.
Lyra Graeca I, Sappho 133

Prayer
. . . κὰτ ἔμον στάλαγμον·
τὸν δ' ἐπιπλάζοντ' ἄμοι φέροιεν
καὶ μελεδώναις.
Sappho (Wharton), 17

Dying Sappho to her daughter Cleis
οὐ γὰρ θέμις ἐν μοισοπόλῳ οἰκίᾳ
θρῆνον θέμεν· οὐκ ἄμμι πρέπει τάδε.
Lyra Graeca I, Sappho 108

Morning
Our songs must end, companions dear,
the east is bright and day is near.

Flowers
Flowers deck both hill and heath
with many a petal-broidered wreath.

Prayer
May driving storm-winds bear away my tears
together with my sorrows and my fears.

Dying Sappho to her daughter Cleis
It is not seemly, daughter, to make moan
here in this house that was the Muses' own.

SAPPHO

QUATRAINS

AND

OTHER SHORT POEMS

*It is Stephanides' translations which are mainly
quatrains; the Greek poetic fragments
of Sappho in this section vary in length
from two to five lines.*

Retrospect
ἐγὼ δὲ φίλημ' ἀβροσύναν, καί μοι τὸ λάμπρον
ἔρος ἀελίω καὶ τὸ κάλον λέλογχεν.

Sappho (Wharton), 79

The boor
κατθάνοισα δὲ κείσεαι οὐδέ τινι μναμοσύνα σέθεν
ἔσσετ' οὐδέποτ' εἰς ὔστερον· οὐ γὰρ πεδέχεις βρόδων
τῶν ἐκ Πιερίας, ἀλλ' ἀφάνης κἠν Ἀΐδα δόμοις
φοιτάσεις πεδ' ἀμαύρων νεκύων ἐπτεποταμένα.

Lyra Graeca I, Sappho 71

Wealth and Virtue
ὁ πλοῦτος δ' ἄνευ ἀρέτας
οὐκ ἀσίνης πάροικος·
ἀ δὲ κρᾶσις ἀμφοτέρων
δαιμονίαν ἄκραν ἔχει·

Lyra Graeca I, Sappho 100

Gold
Διὸς γὰρ πάϊς ἔστ' ὁ χρύσος·
κῆνον οὐ σέες οὐδὲ κῖς
δαρδάπτοισ'· ὁ δὲ δάμναται
καὶ φρένων βροτέαν κράτιστον.

Lyra Graeca I, Sappho 110

Retrospect
A lifetime blessed by Eros
has fallen to my share;
Love has for me the beauty
of the sun through springtime air.

The boor
You will be dead forever; aye, no breath,
no vestige of you to the Earth will cling.
You scorned the roses by the Pierian Spring
and you shall walk the shadowy halls of Death!

Wealth and Virtue
Wealth that knows not Virtue
is a despiteful guest;
but when they both are blended,
by Heaven they are blest.

Gold
Gold is the child of Zeus
that fears no worm or blight;
the strongest mortal mind
is dazzled by its sight.

To her baby daughter Cleis
Ἔστι μοι κάλα πάϊς χρυσίοισιν ἀνθέμοισιν
ἐμφέρην ἔχοισα μόρφαν, Κλεῦις ἀγαπάτα,
ἀντὶ τᾶς ἔγω οὐδὲ Λυδίαν παῖσαν οὐδ' ἐράνναν
Λέσβον ἀγρέην κε . . . . . .

Lyra Graeca I, Sappho 130

Epitaph
Τίμαδος ἄδε κόνις, τὰν δὴ πρὸ γάμοιο θάνοισαν
δέξατο Φερσεφόνας κυάνιος θάλαμος,
ἆς καὶ ἀπυφθιμένας παῖσαι νεόθαγι σιδάρῳ
ἄλικες ἰμμέρταν κρᾶτος ἔθεντο κόμαν.

Lyra Graeca I, Sappho 144

Wine
. . . . . ἔλθε, Κύπρι,
χρυσίαισιν ἐν κυλίκεσσιν ἄβραις
συμμεμείγμενον θαλίαισι νέκταρ
οἰνοχόεισα
τοῖς ἑταίροις τοίσδεσ' ἔμοις τε καὶ σοῖς· . . .

Lyra Graeca I, Sappho 6

To Dica
σὺ δὲ στεφάνοις, ὦ Δίκα, πέρθεσσ' ἐράταις φόβαισιν
ὄρπακας ἀνήτοιο συνέρραισ' ἀπάλαισι χέρσιν·
ταὐάνθεα γὰρ παρπέλεται καὶ Χάριτας μάκαιρας
μᾶλλον προτόρην· ἀστεφανώτοισι δ' ἀπυστρέφονται.

Lyra Graeca I, Sappho 117

QUATRAINS AND OTHER SHORT POEMS

To her baby daughter Cleis
My little daughter, Cleis,
is like a golden flower;
I would not give her for this Isle
or all the Lydian power.

Epitaph
Timas lies here, led on her wedding day
by dread Persephone to her dark nave.
And her companions sheared their lovely locks
and offered them in mourning on her grave.

Wine
Come, Cypris, and in cups of chiselled gold
pour out the wine mixed ready for the feast,
the nectar-flavoured wine. Cup bearer be
to my friends here — and to yourself not least.

To Dica
O Dica, with your dainty hands
weave flowers in your hair's dark strands.
With girls thus decked the Graces stay,
from those uncrowned they turn away.

Complaint

Δέδυκε μὲν ἀ σέλαννα
καὶ Πληΐαδες, μέσαι δὲ
νύκτες, παρὰ δ' ἔρχετ' ὤρα,
ἔγω δὲ μόνα κατεύδω.

Lyra Graeca I, Sappho 111

Love-sickness

Γλύκηα μᾶτερ, οὔ τοι δύναμαι κρέκην τὸν ἴστον
πόθῳ δάμεισα παῖδος βραδίνω δι' 'Αφροδίταν.

Lyra Graeca I, Sappho 135

The apple

οἶον τὸ γλυκύμαλον ἐρεύθεται ἄκρῳ ἐπ' ὔσδῳ
ἄκρον ἐπ' ἀκροτάτῳ, λελάθοντο δὲ μαλοδρόπηες.
οὐ μὰν ἐκλελάθοντ', ἀλλ' οὐκ ἐδύναντ' ἐπίκεσθαι·

Lyra Graeca I, Sappho 150

The altar

Κρῆσσαι νύ ποτ' ὦδ' ἐμμελέως πόδεσσιν
ὤρχηντ' ἀπάλοισ' ἀμφ' ἐρόεντα βῶμον,
πόας τέρεν ἄνθος μάλακον ματεῖσαι.

Lyra Graeca I, Sappho 114

QUATRAINS AND OTHER SHORT POEMS

Complaint
The moon has set, the Pleiades
are sinking from the sky;
the hour is late, the night half gone . . .
yet here, alone, I lie.

Typescript and
Worlds in a Crucible, pages 28 and 29

Love-sickness
Mother, I cannot spin nor weave;
for all day long I pine and grieve
and call my lover without shame —
sweet Aphrodite bears the blame!

The apple
A sweet apple reddens at the tip of the bough;
overlooked by the pickers, it glistens there now.
Perhaps, though, to reach it they all had a try;
it was not forgotten — it dangled too high!

The altar
Thus danced the happy girls of Crete
around the altar long ago;
and, circling with light step, their feet
ruffled the grass below.

The garden
. . . . . ἀμφὶ δ' ὕδωρ
ψῦχρον ὤνεμος κελάδει δι' ὕσδων
μαλίνων, αἰθυσσομένων δὲ φύλλων
κῶμα κατάρρει·
Lyra Graeca I, Sappho 4

Bluebells
οἴαν τὰν ὐάκινθον ἐν ὄρρεσι ποίμενες ἄνδρες
πόσσι καταστείβοισι, χάμαι δ' ἔτι πορφύρα ἄνθη.
Lyra Graeca I, Sappho 151

The cicada
. . . πτερύγων δ' ὐπακακχέει
λιγύραν ἀοίδαν, ὄποτα φλόγι
ὀ θέος κατέτᾳ γάαν
ἐπιπεπτάμενος καταύγῃ . . .
Lyra Graeca I, Sappho 94

Evening
Ἔσπερε πάντα φέρων, ὄσα φαίνολις ἐσκέδασ' αὔως
φέρεις ὄϊν,
φέρεις αἶγα, φέρεις ἀπὺ ϝὸν μάτερι παῖδα.
Lyra Graeca I, Sappho 149

The garden
Through channel-troughs of apple-wood
I hear the singing waters flow;
and from the rustling leaves sweet sleep
drifts down on me below.

Typescript and *Worlds in a Crucible,* page 28

Bluebells
The shepherds lead their flock to grass
and crush the bluebells as they pass;
the distant mountains drink their hue
and glimmer back a deeper blue.

The cicada
From underneath its wings
it pours a shrill, sweet call,
when on the dazzled earth
the summer sunbeams fall.

Evening
O Evening, you bring back from everywhere
all that the Morning scattered here and there.
You bring the flocks back to the waiting farms,
you bring the child home to its mother's arms.

Moonlight

Ἄστερες μὲν ἀμφὶ κάλαν σελάνναν
ἂψ ἀπυκρύπτοισι φάεννον εἶδος,
ὅπποτα πλήθοισα μάλιστα λάμπησ'
ἀργυρία γᾶν.

Lyra Graeca I, Sappho 3

Alcaeus and Sappho

Ἰόπλοκ' ἄγνα μελλιχόμειδε Σάπφοι,
θέλω τι ϝείπην ἀλλά με κωλύει αἴδως.

Lyra Graeca I, Alcaeus 124

αἰ δ' ἦχες ἔσλων ἴμμερον ἢ κάλων
καὶ μή τι ϝείπην γλῶσσ' ἐκύκα κάκον,
αἴδως κεν οὐκί σ' ἦχεν ὄππατ',
ἀλλ' ἔλεγες περὶ τῶ δικαίως.

Lyra Graeca I, Sappho 119

To Atthis

Ἠράμαν μὲν ἔγω σέθεν, Ἄτθι, πάλαι ποτά,
ἆς ἔμ' ἀνθεμόεσσ' ἔτι παρθενία σὺ δὲ
σμίκρα μοι πάϊς ἔμμεν ἐφαίνεο κἄχαρις.

Lyra Graeca I, Sappho 48

Moonlight

The stars around the lovely Moon
flicker and shine less bright
when she, full-orbed upon the Earth
sprinkles her silver light.

Alcaeus and Sappho

ALCAEUS TO SAPPHO
Sweet-eyed Sappho, to you I come;
but bashfulness has made me dumb.

SAPPHO TO ALCAEUS
Had you desired the good and fair
and in you evil had no lair,
you would not, shame-faced, thus beseech,
but frankly and with fearless speech.

To Atthis

I loved you, Atthis, at the time
when you seemed but an awkward child,
and I was in my girlhood's prime.

To a friend
ὄττα γάρ κ' ἐνάντιον εἰσίδω σε
τόττ' ἔμοι οὐ φύνν' Ἑρμιόνα τεαύτα
φαίνεται, ξάνθᾳ δ' Ἑλένᾳ σ' ἐΐσκην
ἔστιν ἔπεικες . . .

Lyra Graeca I, Sappho 44

The return

Ἦλθες· κεῦ ἐποίησας· ἔγω δέ σε
μαόμαν, ὂν δ' ἔφλαξας ἔμαν φρένα
καυομέναν πόθῳ· χαῖρ' ἄμμι, χαῖρε

πόλλα καὶ ϝισάριθμα τόσῳ χρόνῳ
ἀλλάλαν ἀπελείφθημεν.

Lyra Graeca I, Sappho 89

Gorgo
. . . . . μάλα δὴ κεκορημένοις
Γόργως . . . . .

Lyra Graeca I, Sappho 55

QUATRAINS AND OTHER SHORT POEMS

To a friend
I look upon your face and see
a lovelier Hermione,
for you possess a beauty rare
like Helen of the golden hair.

The return

You came. And you did well to come;
for in my heart you lit a fire
that had yourself as its desire.

A hundred welcomes on this day
for every hour you stayed away.

Gorgo
Gorgo . . . I am sick of her!

Worlds in a Crucible, page 28

SAPPHO

LONGER POEMS

After the marriage ceremony

Ὄλβιε γάμβρε, σοὶ μὲν δὴ γάμος, ὡς ἄραο
ἐκτετέλεστ', ἔχεις δὲ πάρθενον, ἂν ἄραο·
Lyra Graeca I, Sappho 155

μελλίχιος δ' ἐπ' ἰμμέρτῳ κέχυται προσώπῳ . . .
Lyra Graeca I, Sappho 156

. . . σοὶ χάριεν μὲν εἶδος
κὤππατα μελλιχόχροα
νύμφ', ἔρος δὲ τέῳ κάλῳ
περκέχυται προσώπῳ,
καί σε τέτικεν ἐξόχως
Ἀφρόδιτα . . .
Lyra Graeca I, Sappho 158

The farewell

αἶσ' ἔγων ἔφαν· Ἄγαναι γύναικες,
οἶα μεμνάσεσθ' ἄï μέχρι γήρας
ὄττιν' ἄμμες ἐν νεότατι λάμπρα
συνεπόημμεν·

ἄγνα μὲν γὰρ καὶ κάλα πόλλ' ἐν αὔτᾳ
δράσαμεν· πόλιν δ' ἀπυλιππανοίσαν
σφῶïν ὀξείαις δάκεν ἴμμερός μοι
θῦμον ἄσαισι.
Lyra Graeca I, Sappho 43

After the marriage ceremony

O groom, the wedding-feast is past,
the girl you sought is yours at last,
her face is rosy with love's gleam.

"Sweet bride, your body is my dream,
your eyes a honied glance distill,
and Eros pours his golden light
upon your limbs to make them bright.

"For it was Aphrodite's will
to lavish on you all her skill."

The farewell

I said: "O honoured women friends,
when in old age Life's journey ends,
you will recall each happy day
we spent with youth to guide our way.

"Our dawns arose in holy light,
with love and beauty till the night;
and, at this hour when you depart,
a sharp-toothed longing gnaws my heart."

To Aphrodite of Knossos

δεῦρύ μ' ἐκ Κρήτας ἐπὶ τόνδε ναῦον
ἄγνον, ὄππαι τοι χάριεν μὲν ἄλσος
μαλίαν, βῶμοι δὲ τεθυμιάμε-
νοι λιβανώτωι·

ἐν δ' ὕδωρ ψῦχρον κελάδει δι' ὔσδων
μαλίνων, βρόδοισι δὲ παῖς ὀ χῶρος
ἐσκίαστ', αἰθυσσομένων δὲ φύλλων
κῶμα καταίρει·

ἐν δὲ λείμων ἰππόβοτος τέθαλεν
ἠρίνοισιν ἄνθεσιν, αἰ δ' ἄηται
μέλλιχα πνέοισιν . . . . .
. . . . . .

ἔνθα δὴ σὺ . . . ...ἔλοισα Κύπρι
χρυσίαισιν ἐν κυλίκεσσιν ἄβρως
ὀμμεμείχμενον θαλίαισι νέκταρ
οἰνοχόαισον

Sappho and Alcaeus (Page), Sappho, Fr. 2

To Aphrodite of Knossos

O Aphrodite, speed from distant Crete
to grace your temple here, where apple-trees
surround an altar from which rising smoke
    drifts on the breeze.

Here roses cast their shadows on the ground
and cooling founts reflect the smiling skies,
and whispering leaves drip down a healing sleep
    on weary eyes.

Here is a meadow where proud horses graze,
and flowers of the spring forever bloom,
where anis trodden underfoot exhales
    its sharp perfume.

And here, O Lady Aphrodite, pour
Love's holy nectar into cups of gold,
to fill them to the brim with lasting joy
    for young and old.

Sappho's lament to Aphrodite

Ποικιλόθρον' ἀθάνατ' Ἀφρόδιτα,
παῖ Δίος δολόπλοκα, λίσσομαί σε·
μή μ' ἄσαισι μηδ' ὀνίαισι δάμνα,
πότνια, θῦμον,

ἀλλὰ τυίδ' ἔλθ', αἴ ποτα κἀτέροττα
τὰς ἔμας αὔδως ἀΐοισα πήλυι
ἔκλυες, πάτρος δὲ δόμον λίποισα
χρύσιον ἦλθες

ἄρμ' ὑπασδεύξαισα, κάλω δέ σ' ἆγον
ὤκεε στροῦθω προτὶ γᾶν μέλαιναν
πύκνα δίννεντε πτέρ' ἀπ' ὀρράνω αἴθε-
ρος διὰ μέσσω,

αἶψα δ' ἐξίκοντο· σὺ δ', ὦ μάκαιρα,
μειδιάσαισ' ἀθανάτῳ προσώπῳ
ἤρε' ὄττι δηῦτε πέπονθα, κὤττι
δηῦτε κάλημι,

κὤττ' ἔμω μάλιστα θέλω γένεσθαι
μαινόλᾳ θύμῳ· τίνα δηῦτε πείθω
καὶ σ' ἄγην ἐς ϝὰν φιλότατα; τίς τ', ὦ
Ψάπφ', ἀδικήει;

καὶ γὰρ αἰ φεύγει, ταχέως διώξει,
αἰ δὲ δῶρα μὴ δέκετ', ἀλλὰ δώσει,
αἰ δὲ μὴ φίλει, ταχέως φιλήσει
κωὒκ ἐθέλοισα·

CONTINUED

LONGER POEMS

Sappho's lament to Aphrodite

Immortal Aphrodite, rainbow-throned,
child of great Zeus and weaver of sweet wiles;
do not allow distress to crush my soul,
but greet me with your smiles.

Come to my aid, if ever in the past
you listened to my songs at eventide;
and, starting from your father's golden halls,
you hastened to my side,

brought hither in your chariot, ready yoked,
by gleaming birds whose swiftly fluttering skeins
skimmed over the dark earth amid the void
of heavenly domains.

And, as in those past times, O Blessed One,
you asked me in your sweet celestial speech
what was the cause of all my suffering,
why did I now beseech,

and what it was I needed to appease
my frantic heart. You said: "Whom must I bow
to your demanding love? O Sappho, tell . . .
Who brings you sorrow now?

"For even if she flees, she will return;
rejected gifts, she will with gifts requite;
and though she spurns your love, soon will she love —
her very self despite!"

CONTINUED

ἔλθε μοι καὶ νῦν, χάλεπαν δὲ λῦσον
ἐκ μερίμναν, ὄσσα δέ μοι τέλεσσαι
θῦμος ἰμμέρρει, τέλεσον, σὺ δ' αὔτα
σύμμαχος ἔσσο.

Lyra Graeca I, Sappho 1

To a dream

Ὄνοιρε, μελαίνας τέκος ὦ νύκτος, ὃς ἔγγυς αὔως
φοίταις ὄτα τ' ὔπνος βρόχυς ἤδη βλεφάροισιν ἄμμοις,

γλύκυς θέος, ἦ δεῖν' ὀνίας μ' ἄλγε' ἔδειξας αἴ κε
ζὰ χῶρις ἔχην τὰν δύναμιν τόν τε πόθον ταλάσσω.

ἔλπις δέ μ' ἔχει μὴ πεδέχην τῶν πρό μ' ἔειπες, ἀλλὰ
μηδὲν μακάρων ἐλδομέναν οὐκὶ λάβην διδόντων.

οὐ γάρ κ' ἔον οὔτως ἄνοον παίδιον ὡς φέροισαν
ἀθύρματα κάλλιστα φίλαν μάτερ' ἀπυστράφεσθαι·

γένοιτο δέ μοι πὰρ μακάρων καῖρος ὄτω ποθήω,
τοῖς πάντας ἀοίδαισι τόσαις καὶ χορίαισ' ἔτισα.

Lyra Graeca Ia, Appendix, Sappho 118B

Thus in the same way, free me once again
from grievous care. Accord me what I sigh
and yearn for most. O Queen, do this for me,
and be my strong ally.

To a dream

Dream, child of night-time, you who to me creep
when dawn is near and the sweet God of Sleep
upon my eyelids can no longer dwell,
what pangs of sorrow do you now foretell
if I should dare refuse to keep apart
desire and its fulfilment by the heart?

My fate may not be such as you have warned,
for never in adulthood have I scorned
any of all the joys that came my way.
Nor, as a child, did I dissent to play
with those bright toys (I was not so unwise)
my mother bought me to delight my eyes.

Thus may the gods grant that for which I long,
I who have honoured them with dance and song.

Sappho

Love

Φαίνεταί μοι κῆνος ἴσος θέοισιν
ἔμμεν ὤνηρ ὄττις ἐνάντιός τοι
ἰζάνει καὶ πλάσιον ἆδυ φωνεί-
σας ὐπακούει

καὶ γελαίσας ἰμμέροεν, τὸ δὴ 'μὰν
κάρζαν ἐν στήθεσσιν ἐπεπτόασεν·
ὠς γὰρ ἔς τ' ἴδω, Βρόχε', ὤς με φώνας
οὐδὲν ἔτ' ἴκει,

ἀλλὰ κὰμ μὲν γλῶσσα ϝέαγε, λέπτον
δ' αὔτικα χρῷ πῦρ ὐπαδεδρόμακεν,
ὀππάτεσσι δ' οὐδὲν ὄρημ', ἐπιρρόμ-
βεισι δ' ἄκουαι,

ἀ δέ μ' ἴδρως κακχέεται, τρόμος δὲ
παῖσαν ἄγρη, χλωροτέρα δὲ ποίας
ἔμμι, τεθνάκην δ' ὀλίγω 'πιδεύϝην
φαίνομαι· — ἀλλὰ

πάντα νῦν τολμάτε', ἐπεὶ πένησα.

Lyra Graeca I, Sappho 2

Love

Beyond all other mortals is he blessed,
that man who sits by you and can rejoice
in your sweet laughter and your lilting voice
which causes my heart to flutter in my breast.

For every time I look upon your face
a flame devours my body and my mind;
my tongue can speak no word; my eyes are blind;
and in my ears I hear wild waters race.

I shiver and I burn; I turn as pale
as grass in summer drought; I pant for breath;
I seem to balance on the brink of death;
I feel the life-springs of existence fail —

And yet for you, for you I would dare all! . . .

The departure of Anactoria

Ἄτθι, σοὶ κἄμ᾽ Ἀνακτορία φίλα
πηλόροισ᾽ ἐνὶ Σάρδεσιν
ναίει, πόλλακι τυίδε νῶν ἔχοισα,

ὤς ποτ᾽ ἐζώομεν βίον, ἇς ἔχε
σὲ θέᾳ ϝικέλαν ἀρι-
γνώτᾳ, σᾷ δὲ μάλιστ᾽ ἔχαιρε μόλπᾳ.

νῦν δὲ Λύδαισιν ἐμπρέπεται γυναί-
κεσσιν ὤς ποτ᾽ ἀελίω
δύντος ἀ βροδοδάκτυλος σελάννα

πὰρ τὰ περρέχοισ᾽ ἄστρα, φάος δ᾽ ἐπί-
σχει θάλασσαν ἐπ᾽ ἀλμύραν
ἴσως καὶ πολυανθέμοις ἀρούραις,

ἀ δ᾽ ἐέρσα κάλα κέχυται τεθά-
λαισι δὲ βρόδα κἄπαλ᾽ ἄν-
θρυσκα καὶ μελίλωτος ἀνθεμώδης.

πόλλα δὲ ζαφοίταισ᾽ ἀγάνας ἐπι-
μνάσθεισ᾽ Ἀτθίδος ἰμμέρῳ,
λέπταν ποι φρένα κῆρ᾽ ἄσᾳ βόρηται.

κῆθι τ᾽ ἔλθην ἄμμ᾽ ὀξυβόη· τὰ δ᾽ οὐ
νῶν γ᾽ ἄπυστα νὺξ πολύως
γαρυίει δι᾽ ἄλος παρενρεοίσας.

Lyra Graeca I, Sappho 86

The departure of Anactoria

O Atthis, our dear Anactoria lives
in distant Sardis; but her soul in flight
turns often back to us, and she recalls
the life we led together. In her sight
you still remain the goddess of her choice,
she still remembers you and your embrace,
and how she loved your gentle, lulling voice.

Now there among the Lydian girls she gleams
like the soft-fingered Moon when, in the night,
she dims the stars and pours in equal share
on flowered field and ocean wave her light;
and on each living thing a dewdrop glows
to quicken and to freshen once again
the melilot, the chervil and the rose.

And often Anactoria brings to mind
her darling Atthis, and within her breast
a longing weighs upon her mournful heart,
a deep regret that will not let her rest.
She calls aloud for us to come! And we
can hear her sighs — for Night has many tongues
to bear her cry to us across the sea.

To Anactoria

Οἱ μὲν ἱππήων στρότον οἱ δὲ πέσδων
οἱ δὲ νάων φαῖσ' ἐπὶ γᾶν μέλαιναν
ἔμμεναι κάλιστον· ἔγω δὲ κῆν ὄτ-
τω τις ἔραται.

πάγχυ δ' εὔμαρες σύνετον πόησαι
πάντι τοῦτ'· ἀ γὰρ πόλυ περσκόπεισα
κάλλος ἀνθρώπων Ἑλένα τὸν ἄνδρα
κρίννε κάλιστον

ὂς τὸ πὰν σέβας Τροΐας ὄλεσσε,
κωὔδε παῖδος οὐδὲ φίλων τοκήων
μᾶλλον ἐμνάσθη, ἀλλὰ παράγαγ' αὔταν
πῆλε φίλεισαν

Ὤρος· εὔκαμπτον γὰρ ἀεὶ τὸ θῆλυ
αἴ κέ τις κούφως τὸ πάρον νοήσῃ·
ἄμμε νυν, Ϝανακτορία, τὺ μέμναι-
σ' οὐ παρεοίσαις,

τᾶς κε βολλοίμαν ἔρατόν τε βᾶμα
κἀμάρυγμα λάμπρον ἴδην προσώπω
ἢ τὰ Λύδων ἄρματα κἀν ὄπλοισι
πεσδομάχεντας·

εὖ μὲν ἴδμεν οὐ δύνατον γένεσθαι
λῷστ' ὂν ἀνθρώποις· πεδέχην δ' ἄρασθαι
τῶν πέδηχόν ἐστι βρότοισι λῷον
ἢ λελάθεσθαι.

Lyra Graeca I, Sappho 38

LONGER POEMS

To Anactoria

Some claim the fairest thing on this dark earth
is charging horse; some foot in close array;
some ships of war. But it is fairer far
        to be in love, I say.

And this can readily be brought to proof:
thus lovely Helen, although she had wed
one of the handsomest of mortal men,
        chose for her mate and fled

with him who brought to naught the pride of Troy.
Nor thought she fondly of her child, and all
the home and friends that she had left behind;
        for love held her in thrall.

Aye, easily is woman by desire
and by a moment's passion led astray . . .
But, Anactoria, keep me still in mind,
        though you be far away.

For I would rather hear your lovèd step,
and your bright glance far sooner would I see
than chariots and phalanxes and all
        the Lydian panoply.

Well do I know that mortals cannot hope
to win their every heart ambition — yet
to mourn a once-shared love is sweeter woe
        than, coldly, to forget.

Farewell to Atthis

Ἄτθιδ' οὔποτ' ἄρ' ὄψομαι,
τεθνάκην δ' ἀδόλως θέλω.
ἄ με ψισδομένα κατελίππανεν

πόλλα, καὶ τόδ' ἔειπέ μοι·
Ὤιμ', ὡς δεῖνα πεπόνθαμεν·
Ψάπφ' ἦ μάν σ' ἀέκοισ' ἀπυλιππάνω.

τὰν δ' ἔγω τάδ' ἀμειβόμαν·
Χαίροισ' ἔρχεο κἄμεθεν
μέμναισ'· οἶσθα γὰρ ὥς τ' ἐπεδήπομεν.

αἰ δὲ μή, ἀλλά σ' ἔγω θέλω
ὄμναισαι τὰ σὺ λάθεαι,
ὄσσ' ἄμμες φίλα καὶ κάλ' ἐπάσχομεν·

πόλλοις ἆ στεφάνοις ἴων
καὶ βρόδων γλυκίων γ' ὔμοι
κὰπ πλόκων πὰρ ἔμοι περεθήκαο,

καὶ πόλλαις ὐπαθύμιδας
πλέκταις ἀμφ' ἀπάλᾳ δέρᾳ
ἀνθέων ἔκατον πεποημμέναις,

καὶ πόλλῳ νέαρον σὺ χρῶ
βρενθείῳ προχόῳ μύρῳ
ἐξαλείψαο καὶ βασιληΐῳ,

καὶ στρώμνας ἔπι κημένα
ἀπάλαν πὰν ὀνηάτων
ἐξίης πόθον ἠδὲ πότων γλυκίων . . .

Lyra Graeca I, Sappho 83

LONGER POEMS

Farewell to Atthis

No more shall I see Atthis; and in truth
I wish that I were dead. She said to me,
amid her tears, "Ah, what a fate is ours!
Sappho, I leave your side unwillingly."
And I replied: "May gladness go with you,
but not forgetfulness. Keep in your mind
the many bonds of love that link us two.

"Retain a memory of past delights;
of how you sat by me with roses crowned,
while necklets woven of a hundred blooms
were twined to grace your snowy throat around.
Remember how your slender limbs would shine
with costly myrrh, and how we two would share
the orchard's bounties and the spicèd wine."

On Gongyla's departure

Τὰν ταχίσταν, ὦ κέλομαί σ' ὄνελθε,
Γόγγυλα βρόδανθι λάβοισα μάνδυν
γλακτίναν· σὲ δηῦτε πόθος τις ἆμος
ἀμφιπόταται

τὰν κάλαν· ἀ γὰρ κατάγωγις αὖτα
ἐπτόαισ' ἴδοισαν ἔγω δὲ χαίρω.
καὶ γὰρ αὖτα δή ποτ' ἐμεμφόμαν τὰν
Κυπρογένηαν·

τᾶς ἄραμαι μὴ χάριν ἀβφέρην μοι
τοῦτο τὦπος, ἀλλά σε, τὰν μάλιστα
βόλλομαι θνάταν κατίδην γυναίκων
ἂψ πάλιν ἔλκην.

Lyra Graeca I, Sappho 4

On Gongyla's departure

Come back to me as swiftly as you can,
my sweet Gongyla, in your milk-white dress.
My longing seeks you out and flutters round
        in soft unseen caress.

Would I could watch your homing ship's return —
I thrill already thinking of that day,
I who once railed at Cypris when she bore
        you whom I love away.

Now may those hasty words of mine not cost
me her good-will or lay a curse on me;
but may they draw my darling to my side,
        whom I wish most to see.

Sappho to her pupils

Ἀτίετε Μοίσαν βαθυκόλπων κάλα δῶρα, παῖδες,
Πρώταν σ' ἐνέποισαι ὦ φίλ', ἄοιδον λιγύραν χελύνναν

ἐρέψομεν· ἦρ' οὐκί μ' ἄπαντα χρόα γῆρας ἤδη
συνέσπασε, λεῦκαί τ' ἐγένοντο τρίχες ἐκ μελαίναν,

παῦροί τέ μ' ἔδοντες περέασιν, γόνα δ' οὐ φέροισι
δέμας πεδὰ τῶ πρόσθ' ἐσυνόρχησθ' ἴσα νεβρίοισιν

ἐλαφροτάτοισι ζοίων; ἀλλὰ τί κεν ποείην;
οὐ γὰρ θέος αὖτος δύνατ' ὄττ' οὐ δύνατον γενέσθαι,

νημέρτεα δ' ὦστ' ἄμμι πέδεισι βροδόπαχυν αὔων
νὺξ ἀστερόεσσα δνόφον εἰς τάσχατα γᾶς φέροισα

οὕτως Ἀΐδας πὰν πεδέπων ζοῖον ὕμως ἔμαρψε,
κωὔτ' ἤθελεν Ὀρφῇϊ δίδων κεδνοτάταν ἄκοιτιν

παῖσάν τε γύναικ' αἷι κατίσχην φθιμέναν νομίσδει
αἱ καί σφ' ἐπαοίδαισι συνώρω ἠϋλύραις ὀπάσδοι.

ἔγω δὲ φίλημμ' ἀβροσύναν, κέκλυτε τοῦτο, καί μοι
τὸ λάμπρον ἔρος τὠελίω καὶ τὸ κάλον λέλογχε·

ἐπ' ἴλεον οὖν πρίν με δέην οὐκ ἀπύβαν νόημμι
φίλεισα δὲ σὺνν ὔμμι φιλείσαισι βίον διάξω·

καὶ νῦν τόδ' ἄλις μοι πέλετ', οὐδὲ πλέον οὖν κ' ἀραίμαν·

Lyra Graeca Ia, Appendix, Sappho 118

LONGER POEMS

Sappho to her pupils

You slight the Muses, children, when you say:
"We'll crown Sappho for her sweet voice today."

Do you not see that Time my face has lined,
and snowy hairs among the black entwined?

Do you not notice that my weary feet
can no more bear me as of old when, fleet,

I outstripped in the dance, as though on wings,
the fawns, those nimblest of all living things?

But thus it is. What can I do, my dears?
Even the gods cannot turn back the years.

As rosy Dawn is tracked by starry Night,
so Age does ever darken all delight;

and Death would not return to me my life,
who gave not back to Orpheus his sweet wife.

But, children, hear me; even now I long
for gracious living, beauty, joy and song;

I have no wish to die before I need,
or quit this world until it is decreed.

It is enough for me that on this shore
I hold your love — I seek for nothing more.

Sappho greets her pupils

'Επτάξατέ μοι, παῖδες, ἄκα τὰς μεγάλας ὔπισθα
δάφνας, ὄτα τὰν ἒπ πόλιος χθίσδος ὄδον πάρηα,

πὰν δ' ἄδιον αἶψ' ἢ τὸ πάρος γέντο κατ' ὔμμ' ἰδοίσᾳ·
ἢ κῆνον ἔλον διψελίοισιν πότον ὀππάτεσσι·

καὶ ταῖσι μὲν ἄλλαις ἐδόκην ὡς ἄλαλός τις εὔθυς
ὀδοίπορος, ἂν τ' ἔμμι γυναίκων ἀμέλης γένεσθαι·

μύγις δέ ποτ' εἰσάϊον· ἔλυσδε δέ μ' ὦτα ῥόμβος,
ψύχα δ' ἀγαπάτα συνάγρεισα φρένας ἐκπότατο.

τέαυτα δέ νυν ἔμμορε μέν, κἄμ' ἐδόκη πρὸς ὔμμε
ἴκεσθ', ἄγαναι παῖδες, ἴοισαν δ' ἀπυκλαυίσαισαι

ἔφθατε· κάλαν δὲ ζὰ θύρας ὄψιν ἔγω κάτειδον
τὰ τ' ἔμματα καὔτ' ὔμμα γ' ἔμαν κάρζαν ἐπεπτόασαν.

Lyra Graeca Ia, Appendix, Sappho 118A

Sappho greets her pupils

You hid yourselves, O children, crouching down
behind the laurel, as I left for town.

And when I saw you, brighter grew the skies;
I drank my fill of you with thirsting eyes.

The other women watched me stare and gawk . . .
I saw them not, I heard no more their talk;

for, my belovèd pupils, at your sight
my eyes and ears were spellbound with delight.

Sappho refuses to marry again

αἰ δέ μοι γάλακτος ἐπάβολ' ἦσκε
τωῦθατ' ἢ παίδων δόλοφυν ποήσει
ἀρμένα, τότ' οὐ τρομέροις πρὸς ἄλλα
λέκτρα καὶ πόσσι

ἠρχόμαν· νῦν δὲ χρόα γῆρας ἤδη
μυρίαν ἄμμον ρύτιν ἀμφιβάσκει,
κωὒ πρὸς ἄμμ' Ἔρος πέταται διώκων
ἀλγεσίδωρος.

Lyra Graeca I, Sappho 42

Sappho refuses to marry again

If my two breasts could still be tense with milk
and if my womb the pangs of birth could know,
then gladly to another marriage bed
with eager, trembling footsteps would I go.
But, as it is, Old Age across my face
has drawn a thousand wrinkles. — It is plain
that Love is in no haste to seek me out
with his twin gifts of rapture and of pain.

Sappho in exile

Πλάσιον δή μοι κατ' ὄναρ παρείη,
πότνι' Ἥρα, σὰ χαρίεσσα μόρφα,
τὰν ἀράταν Ἀτρέϊδαι ϝίδον κλῆ-
τοι βασίληες

ἐκτελέσσαντες Τροΐας ὄλεθρον·
πρῶτα μὲν παρ' ὠκυρόω Σκαμάνδρω
τυίδ' ἀπορμάθεντες ἐπ' οἶκον ἴκην
οὐκ ἐδύναντο,

πρὶν δὲ καὶ Δί' ἀντιάσαι μέγιστον
καὶ Θυώνας ἰμμερόεντα παῖδα.
νῦν δὲ κἄγω, πότνια, λίσσομαί σε
κὰτ τὸ πάροιθεν

ἄγνα καὶ κάλ' ἐν Μυτιλανάαισι
παρθένοις με δρᾶν πάλιν, αἶς χορεύην
ἀμφὶ σαῖσι πόλλ' ἐδίδαξ' ἑόρταις
πόλλα τ' ἀείδην.

ὤς τε νᾶας Ἀτρέϊδαι σὺν ὔμμι
ἆραν Ἰλίω, κέλομαί σε κἄμοι
ἔμμεναι πρὸς οἶκον ἀπυπλεοίσᾳ, Ἥρ'
ἦπι' ἄρωγον.

Lyra Graeca I, Sappho 40

Sappho in exile

May I behold before me in a dream
your gracious form in answer to my plea,
O goddess Hera, whom the noble sons
of Atreus did see

when, after the downfall of warlike Troy,
they could not leave from swift Scamander's shore
to hurry eagerly towards their homes,
till they had bowed before

you and great Zeus, the highest of the gods,
together with Thyone's child divine.
So now, dear Lady, I implore you, hear
once more this prayer of mine:

Let me return to Mytilene's fields
among the maidens whom, in other days,
I taught to dance before your holy shrine
and sing your joyous praise.

As once the ships of the Atridae sailed
from Ilium, saved by your protecting hand,
likewise, O Hera, guard me on my way
to my own native land.

Dying Sappho to Gongyla

ἦρ ἀ . . .
δῆρα το . . .
Γογγύλα τ' ἔφατ'· Οὔ τί πᾳ τόδ' ἔγνως;

ἦ τι σᾶμ' ἐθέλης δεικνύναι τέαις
παῖσι; Μάλιστ', ἀμειβόμαν ἔγω. Ἔρ-
μας γ' εἰσῆλθ'· ἐπὶ δὲ βλέποισ' ἔγω ϝε

εἶπον· Ὦ δέσποτ' ἔππαν ἀπωλόμαν·
οὐ μὰ γὰρ μάκαιραν ἔγω θέαν
οὐδὲν ἄδομ' ἔπαρθ' ἄγαν ἔτ' ὄλβῳ,

κατθάνην δ' ἴμμερός τις ἄγρεσέ με·
λῶ στᾶσ' εἰς δροσόεντ' ἄγρον σέ μ' οἶ
'Ατρήδαν 'Αγαμέμνον' ἄγαγες πρὶν

πάν τε ταΐρητον ἄνθος 'Αχαιίων.
χρῆ δὲ τοῦτ' ἀπυλιππάνην με φαῦ-
ος, ἄτις ὀ . . .

Lyra Graeca I, Sappho 85

Dying Sappho to Gongyla

I said, "It will be soon." Gongyla said:
"How can you tell? Have you received a sign?"
"Aye," I replied, "Hermes stood by my bed;
I turned and spoke to him: 'O Lord divine,
it is the end. I take no more delight
in all that pleased me best beneath the sky.
A longing now pursues me day and night,
an eagerness to close my eyes and die.

'But, Lord, I beg of you to set me down
in those same dewy fields where, by your power,
you guided Agamemnon and the flower
of the Achaeans in their past renown.'"

Setting Pleiades

The Pleiades that Sappho sang
still glimmer in the sky,
and sometimes with the setting Moon
I watch them sink and die.

I wonder then if lovers gaze,
as once, upon their light
to augur if they, too, must yearn
alone all through the night.

Theodore Stephanides
Cities of the Mind, page 34

SHORT POEMS

OF OTHER

ANCIENT GREEK AUTHORS

Life

Σκηνὴ πᾶς ὁ βίος καὶ παίγνιον· ἢ μάθε παίζειν,
τὴν σπουδὴν μεταθείς, ἢ φέρε τὰς ὀδύνας.

Greek Anthology IV, Book X, 72

Sepulchral epigram

Ἀστέρας πρὶν μὲν ἔλαμπες ἐνὶ ζωοῖσιν Ἑῷος·
νῦν δὲ θανὼν λάμπεις Ἕσπερος ἐν φθιμένοις.

Greek Anthology II, Book VII, 670

Laïs' mirror

Ἡ σοβαρὸν γελάσασα καθ' Ἑλλάδος, ἥ ποτ' ἐραστῶν
ἑσμὸν ἐπὶ προθύροις Λαῒς ἔχουσα νέων,
τῇ Παφίῃ τὸ κάτοπτρον· ἐπεὶ τοίη μὲν ὁρᾶσθαι
οὐκ ἐθέλω, οἵη δ' ἦν πάρος οὐ δύναμαι.

Greek Anthology I, Book VI, 1

Life

This life's a stage, a jest. Then learn to play:
endure your pain and cast all cares away!

Palladas of Alexandria, circa 400 AD

Sepulchral epigram

A Morning Star, you gladdened us in life;
and, Evening Star, you now console the dead.

Attributed to Plato, 4th century BC

Laïs' mirror

I, Laïs, who once smiled so proud
upon my lovers' eager crowd,
to Aphrodite dedicate
this mirror I have come to hate . . .
For what it tells I dare not know
and what I was it cannot show.

Attributed to Plato

The Tenth Muse

'Εννέα τὰς Μούσας φασίν τινες· ὡς ὀλιγώρως·
ἠνίδε καὶ Σαπφὼ Λεσβόθεν ἡ δεκάτη.

Greek Anthology III, Book IX, 506

Appearance

ἔκδεξαί με μικρόν, φαντασία· ἄφες ἴδω τίς εἶ
καὶ περὶ τίνος . . .

Epictetus (Schenkl), page 188

(No specific source for the last two lines of Stephanides'
quatrain has been identified. See the Notes.)

The astronomer

Οἶδ' ὅτι θνατὸς ἐγὼ καὶ εφάμερος· ἀλλ' ὅταν ἄστρων
μαστεύω πυκινὰς ἀμφιδρόμους ἕλικας,
οὐκέτ' ἐπιψαύω γαίης ποσίν, ἀλλὰ παρ' αὐτῷ
Ζανὶ θεοτρεφέος πίμπλαμαι ἀμβροσίης.

Greek Anthology III, Book IX, 577

OTHER ANCIENT GREEK AUTHORS

The Tenth Muse

                        Some say
there are Nine Muses — let them think again,
for Lesbian Sappho should be hailed the Tenth!

                        Attributed to Plato
        Typescript and *Worlds in a Crucible*, page 28

Appearance

Appearance, wait for me a little breath,
let me see what you are and represent;
give me just time to winnow Life from Death
and disentangle Earth and Firmament.

                After Epictetus, *circa 130 AD*

The astronomer

A mortal I — but when I trace
the planetary paths through space,
no more upon the earth I stand
for I am raised to God's right hand!

           Claudius Ptolemaeus, *circa AD 150*
     Typescript and *Cities of the Mind*, page 58

The lover

'Ηρίστησα μὲν ἰτρίου λεπτοῦ μικρὸν ἀποκλάς,
οἴνου δ' ἐξέπιον κάδον, νῦν δ' ἀβρῶς ἐρόεσσαν
ψάλλω πηκτίδα τῇ φίλῃ κωμάζων Πολιάγρῃ.

Lyra Graeca II, Anacreon 18

The exile

Εἰ καί σευ πολύφωνος ἀεὶ πίμπλησιν ἀκουὰς
ἢ φόβος εὐχομένων, ἢ χάρις εὐξαμένων,
Ζεῦ Σχερίης ἐφέπων ἱερὸν πέδον, ἀλλὰ καὶ ἡμέων
κλῦθι, καὶ ἀψευδεῖ νεῦσον ὑποσχεσίῃ,
ἤδη μοι ξενίης εἶναι πέρας, ἐν δέ με πάτρῃ
ζώειν, τῶν δολιχῶν παυσάμενον καμάτων.

Greek Anthology III, Book IX, 7

Epitaph for Leonidas and his Three Hundred

Ὦ ξεῖν', ἄγγειλον Λακεδαιμονίοις ὅτι τῇδε
κείμεθα τοῖς κείνων ῥήμασι πειθόμενοι.

Greek Anthology II, Book VII, 249
(compare Lyra Graeca II, Simonides 119)

The lover

I took (for thus do poets lunch)
a sip of wine, a crust to munch;
and, as my true-love hurried by,
we sang her praise, my lyre and I.

Anacreon, 520 BC

The exile

Zeus, you who rule Corcyra's holy shore,
your ears must ring to cries of pain or bliss
from those who at your altar-side implore
or hymn your praise. But, Zeus, still grant me this:
pray shorten my exile that I, the rover,
may see my native isle, my travels over.

Julius Polyaenus of Sardis, 1st century BC

Epitaph for Leonidas and his Three Hundred

O Stranger, go tell the Lacedaemonians
that here we lie obedient to our laws.

Simonides of Ceos, 556–467 BC
Island Trails, page 18

Epitaph to the Spartan dead at Plataea

Ἄσβεστον κλέος οἵδε φίλῃ περὶ πατρίδι θέντες
κυάνεον θανάτου ἀμφεβάλοντο νέφος.
οὐδὲ τεθνᾶσι θανόντες, ἐπεί σφ' ἀρετὴ καθύπερθε
κυδαίνουσ' ἀνάγει δώματος ἐξ 'Αΐδεω.

Greek Anthology II, Book VII, 251
(compare *Lyra Graeca* II, Simonides 126)

Epitaph to a Maltese watch-dog

Τῇδε τὸν ἐκ Μελίτης ἀργὸν κύνα φησὶν ὁ πέτρος
ἴσχειν, Εὐμήλου πιστότατον φύλακα.
Ταῦρόν μιν καλέεσκον, ὅτ' ἦν ἔτι· νῦν δὲ τὸ κείνου
φθέγμα σιωπηραὶ νυκτὸς ἔχουσιν ὁδοί.

Greek Anthology II, Book VII, 211

The hypochondriac's epitaph

(No Greek source has been traced. See the Notes.)

Epitaph to the Spartan dead at Plataea

Upon their own dear land eternal fame
they shed and passed into death's sombre cloud.
Yet, dying, they died not; valour's acclaim
frees them, immortal, from their earthly shroud.

Simonides of Ceos
Typescript and *Island Trails*, page 18

Epitaph to a Maltese watch-dog

The snow-white Maltese dog beneath this loam
was once the guardian of Eumelus' home;
his faithful bark that voiced and gave delight
now echoes down the empty ways of Night.

Tymnes *in The Greek Anthology, 2nd century BC*

The hypochondriac's epitaph

See! I was right in spite of all their jeers.
I who this grave now fill:
I kept on telling them for eighty years
that I was *really* ill.

?Anonymous
Autumn Gleanings, page 130

NOTES ON THE POEMS OF SAPPHO

DISTICHS

5. *The doves*. There is no mention of doves in the surviving line-and-a-half of the Greek, but the source, a *scholium* on Pindar, introduces this fragment as what Sappho says "about the doves". In the second line, "do" has been added before "droop" by the editor for the sake of the metre; its omission from the *Typescript* may well have been an accident.

5. *The river*. The first line is Stephanides' invention to provide a context for the second, which translates a single surviving line of Greek. In the *Typescript* the first line is in brackets.

7. *To the Muses* and *Invocation*. In the Greek sources, the first of these is without title and it is the second which has the title "To the Muses" (*eis tas Mousas*).

7. *The girdle*. "From some far Lydian town" is the first of four references to Lydia in these poems. Lydia, in Sappho's time, was an extensive kingdom in Asia Minor (the mainland to the east of Sappho's island of Lesbos) and it seems to be associated by her with wealth and power. See the references to "Lydian power" (*To her baby daughter Cleis*, page 15) and "Lydian panoply" (*To Anactoria*, page 39).

9. *Dying Sappho to her daughter Cleis*. In the Greek source the title is given as "To her [*literally* the] daughter" (*pros tên thugatera*). What remains of the original poem does not refer to a daughter at all, nor to the occasion of grief; but Maximus of Tyre (2nd century AD), in whose *Dissertations* this fragment is preserved, says that "Socrates reproved [his wife] Xanthippe for weeping when he was dying, as did Sappho her daughter".

QUATRAINS AND OTHER SHORT POEMS

13. *Retrospect.* Wharton's edition of Sappho has been used here because it provides a two-line fragment which corresponds fairly closely to what Stephanides has translated. After Wharton's time a much larger fragment was discovered in the Oxyrhynchus papyri, where the lines provided by Wharton appear in the slightly longer eighth distich of the poem which Stephanides calls *Sappho to her pupils* (pages 44–45). In *Retrospect*, while ignoring the first four words of Wharton's text (translated by Wharton as "I love delicacy"), Stephanides has expanded the remaining ten words into a quatrain by translating key words twice with different meaning. Stephanides' lines 3–4 correspond to (but elaborate) Wharton's prose translation: "and for me Love has the sun's splendour and beauty", where "for me Love has" translates *moi . . . eros . . . lelonchen,* with the verb *lelonchen* taken in its simplified meaning "has come into possession of" (and therefore "has"). In lines 1–2 of the quatrain, with Love here more specifically the Greek god Eros, and the Greek word *eros* expanded into "A lifetime blessed by Eros", Stephanides translates *moi . . . lelonchen* again, but as "has fallen to my share" (literally "to me has fallen as a share"), taking the verb in its basic sense. As part of *Sappho to her pupils* Stephanides translates these words rather differently, and more loosely, ignoring the verb *lelonchen* and without any reference to "Love" or "the sun": "even now I long / for gracious living, beauty, joy and song" ("gracious living" obviously corresponding to "delicacy" in Wharton's rendering of the shorter passage). It may be that the translation of the longer text was made years after the translation of the fragment, and that Stephanides was not aware that one Greek text was included in the other. Alternatively, the loose translation in the longer poem may have been a deliberate strategy to avoid repeating what he had already written in *Retrospect*.

13. *The boor.* As is clear in Greek from the gender of two participles, this is addressed to a woman; and Ancient Greek authors who refer to this poem describe it variously as "to a

woman of no education", "to a wealthy woman", and "to a woman of no refinement of learning"; but also, and perhaps most pertinently, "to one who didn't love poetry", for the Pierian Spring (in southern Macedonia, near Mount Olympus) whose roses the boor scorned, was sacred to the Muses and regarded as a source of knowledge and inspiration.

15. *To her baby daughter Cleis.* In the Greek source the title is simply "To Cleis" (*pros Klëin*). In line 3 "this Isle" replaces "Lesbos" of the restored Greek fourth line.

15. *Epitaph.* The Greek title is "To Timas" (*pros Timada*).

15. *Wine.* The Greek title is "To Aphrodite" (*eis Aphroditên*). "Cypris" is one of the goddess's titles, referring to her association with the island of Cyprus, one of two places where she is said to have "arisen from the foam". The other is the island of Cythera. See also below (31. *Sappho's Lament to Aphrodite*).

15. *To Dica.* The Greek title is "To Mnesidice" (*pros Mnêsidikên*). "Dica" is a diminutive of "Mnesidice". In Greek mythology, the Graces, usually said to be three in number, were the divine patronesses of life's pleasures (compare the nine Muses who each presided over a different art).

17. *Complaint.* The translation was first published in *Worlds in a Crucible* (page 29) as the second of "Four Quatrains", with the heading "*Lament* (Sappho)". The ellipsis at the end of the third line is from the version in Stephanides' poem "The Tenth Muse" (see page 1). I have preferred this to the comma at the end of this line in the *Typescript*. The translation in "The Tenth Muse" differs from that in the *Typescript*, the verbal changes being needed to fit the poem into three iambic pentameters. See also Stephanides' *Setting Pleiades* on page 55, a poem which takes Sappho's *Complaint* as its starting point. The Pleiades are a roughly circular cluster of stars (within the constellation of Taurus) of which the brightest seven were also known to the

Ancient Greeks as the Seven Sisters. The Pleiades are known in modern astronomy as M45.

17. *The altar.* First published in *Worlds in a Crucible* (page 29) as the first of "Four Quatrains", with the heading *"The Altar (Sappho; circa 600 B.C.)"*. Sappho is probably referring to the cult of Aphrodite which for her was, it seems, particularly associated with the island of Crete (compare below: 29. *To Aphrodite of Knossos*). Crete is not regarded as one of the major centres of the cult by modern historians.

19. *The garden.* The less satisfactory version embedded in Stephanides' poem *The Tenth Muse* (page 1) consists essentially of the same words and phrases rearranged to fit into three iambic pentameters. The syllabic count (30) is the same in both versions: 10 + 10 + 10 or 8 + 8 + 8 + 6.

19. *The cicada.* Preserved in the *De elocutione* of Demetrius of Phalerum (4th–3rd century BC), the incomplete Greek lines themselves contain no reference to the cicada, but they are introduced by Demetrius as an example of poetic grace achieved through metaphor "like that of the cicada [*tettix*]".

21. *Alcaeus and Sappho.* In the Greek source the last four lines have the title "to Alcaeus" (*pros Alkaion*). The first two lines are usually included among the fragments of Alcaeus, another lyric poet of Lesbos. It is however possible that Sappho wrote these lines to provide the context for her reply. It is probable that Alcaeus was Sappho's older contemporary, though this has been disputed. For neither of them can precise dates of birth or death be ascertained. Alcaeus' lyrics, like those of Sappho, survive only in partial and fragmentary form.

21. *To Atthis.* The Greek title is the same, *pros Atthida*. Atthis figures in other poems in this selection. *The departure of Anactoria* (page 37) is addressed to Atthis and *Farewell to Atthis* (page 41) records Sappho's last words to Atthis before her departure.

23. *To a friend.* Stephanides has translated only the first complete stanza of an incomplete text that consists of two stanzas preceded by a small part of another. The Greek text provided is only that of the stanza translated. In Greek mythology, Hermione was the daughter of king Menelaus and his wife Helen — "Helen of Troy", who deserted her husband and fled with Paris to Troy. Helen had been considered the most beautiful woman in the world, and her suitors, prior to her choice of Menelaus, had agreed that they would stand by whomever she chose. They were the core of the Achaean alliance that embarked on the Trojan War to reclaim Helen.

23. *Gorgo.* This line is taken from Stephanides' poem "The Tenth Muse" (see page 1). "I am sick of" translates a Greek perfect participle ("sick" or "tired") whose ending is uncertain (possibly *kekorêmenois* or *kekorêmenas*), leaving gender and number unclear, and thus Stephanides' introduction of "I" is reasonable though speculative.

LONGER POEMS

27. *After the marriage ceremony.* In this nine-line poem Stephanides has ingeniously combined three separate fragments of Sappho which occur almost in succession in *Lyra Graeca* I. His first two lines correspond to fragment 155, the third to 156, and the remaining six lines to fragment 158, with the result that the groom addressed in 155 seems to respond, in the translation of 158, to the promptings of the poet.

29. *To Aphrodite of Knossos.* Sappho appears to regard Crete as the home of Aphrodite. See also above (17. *The Altar*). Knossos was the site of the principal Minoan palace on Crete, about 800 years earlier than Sappho. On the relatively recent discovery of the greater part of this poem, see the Introduction, pages xii–xiii.

31. *Sappho's Lament to Aphrodite.* The Greek title is simply "To Aphrodite" (*eis Aphroditên*). Sappho calls Aphrodite "child of great Zeus"; and in one myth she was indeed the daughter of

Zeus and the goddess Dione. In another, though, she was the product of Cronus' castration of his father Uranus ("Sky") and the casting of his genitals into the sea, hence the notion that she was "arisen from the foam" (one explanation of the meaning of *aphrodîtê*, since *aphros* means "foam").

33. *To a dream*. The Greek title is the same, *eis oneiron*.

35. *Love*. See the Introduction (pages x–xi) on the title of this poem, which in the *Typescript* is *To Anactoria*. Stephanides has translated the whole poem, but, while maintaining the separate final line (though taking "And yet" from *alla* in the line before), he has reorganized the four full stanzas of the original into three stanzas.

37. *The departure of Anactoria*. The poem is addressed to Atthis, and the Greek title is "To Atthis" (*pros Atthida*). Stephanides translates the seven three-line stanzas of the Greek into three eight-line stanzas. His first stanza corresponds to the stanzas 1–2 of the Greek, his second to stanzas 3–5, and his third to stanzas 6–7. The last line of the Greek is uncertain, and it appears that Stephanides follows Edmonds' restoration in *Lyra Graeca* I, which contains the phrase *di' alos* ("across the sea"). Sardis was, from the mid-seventh century BC, the capital of Lydia (on which see above: 15. *To her baby daughter Cleis*). "Melilot" (from Greek *melilôtos*, meaning "honey-lotus") is the name of a group of plants with clusters of small sweet-smelling white or yellow flowers, also known as sweet clover; "chervil" that of plants of the genus *Anthriscus* (*anthruska* in the Greek text, stanza 5, lines 2–3), with small white flowers and aniseed-flavoured leaves. The leaves are used as a culinary herb.

39. *To Anactoria*. This is the Greek title (*pros Anaktorian*). In the *Typescript* the title is *Love*. See the Introduction (pages x–xi) for the explanation of the reversal of the titles *To Anactoria* and *Love*. On Helen, see above (23. *To a friend*). Here "one of the handsomest of mortal men" refers to her husband Menelaus; and "him who brought to nought the pride of Troy" refers to

Paris. His abduction of Helen led to the Trojan War, in which Troy was eventually taken by the Achaeans, led by Menelaus (on the Achaeans see below: 53. *Dying Sappho to Gongyla*). The comparison with the "Lydian panoply" is apt, because Lydia is where Anactoria was now living — in the capital, Sardis (see the previous poem, *The departure of Anactoria*, page 37).

41. *Farewell to Atthis.* The Greek title is simply "to Atthis" (*pros Atthida*). Stephanides' first stanza translates stanzas 1-3 of the Greek, his second is a rather condensed version of stanzas 4-8. See also the Introduction, page xii.

43. *On Gongyla's departure.* The Greek title is "to Gongyla" (*pros Gongulēn*), but Stephanides' title in the *Typescript* is "On her daughter's departure from home". It is most unlikely that Gongyla was Sappho's daughter, hence the modification of the title (see Introduction, page x). On Cypris as an epithet of Aphrodite see above (15. *Wine*).

45. *Sappho to her pupils.* Stephanides' ten distichs correspond fairly closely to the nine complete distichs and the final partial distich of the Greek, except that his distichs 3–5 correspond to distichs 3-4 of the Greek, and Greek distich 7 (which expands on the Orpheus theme) is not translated. On the translation of the eighthth distich, see above (13. *Retrospect*). In mythology, Orpheus' wife Eurydice died of a snakebite. Orpheus went down into the Underworld to reclaim her and was allowed to take her back into the world on condition that he did not turn to look at her as she followed him to the surface. Emerging into the light, Orpheus looked back before Eurydice herself had crossed the threshold, and thus lost her.

47. *Sappho greets her pupils.* Stephanides translates the first three distichs of the Greek, omits the third and fourth completely, and finishes with a much-simplified translation of the sixth.

51. *Sappho in exile.* It seems that at some time quite early in her adult life Sappho was exiled to Sicily for political reasons. The

poem is addressed to the goddess Hera (both sister and wife of Zeus) and the Greek title is "To Hera" (*pros Éran*). Atreus was king of Mycenae; his sons were Agamemnon and Menelaus (on whom see notes above: 23. *To a friend*; 39. *To Anaktoria*), who are referred to collectively as the Atridae (the Latin form) or Atreides (Greek). Scamander was the Ancient Greek name of the major river flowing through the plain of Troy, beside which many battles of the Trojan War were fought. Mytilene is the principal town of Lesbos, but also an alternative name for the island itself. Thyone's child is Dionysus or Bacchus (as Stephanides explains in a footnote to this poem in the *Typescript*). Ilium (Greek *Ilion*) is another name for Troy; hence *Iliad* (Greek *Ilias*) as the title of the Homeric epic.

53. *Dying Sappho to Gongyla.* On the title of this poem, see the Introduction, pages ix–x. Stephanides' first stanza corresponds to the first three stanzas of the Greek and the first line of the fourth; his second stanza to the remaining five lines. Hermes, as well as being the messenger of the gods, was also the god who led the souls of the dead into the afterlife. "Those same dewy fields" refers to the Elysian Fields, the site of a happier afterlife (an alternative to the Underworld) for those, such as heroes, whom the gods chose to reward. At the beginning of the last book of the *Odyssey*, when Hermes brings souls to the "asphodel meadows", they find there already the soul of Agamemnon as well as the souls of Achilles, Patroclus, Antilochus, and Ajax — heroes who had died fighting in the Trojan War and who might well be described as the "flower of the Achaeans". In Homer "Achaeans" is one of several terms used to denote the Greeks in general. On the uncertainty of any reference to Agamemnon and the Achaeans at this point in Sappho's poem, see the Introduction, page xii.

NOTES ON THE SHORT POEMS OF OTHER ANCIENT GREEK AUTHORS

59. *Laïs' mirror.* This could refer to either of two famous *hetairai* (courtesans): Laïs of Corinth (late fifth century BC) and Laïs of Hyccara (early fourth century BC).

61. *Appearance.* This quatrain, described by Stephanides as "After Epictetus", is derived from prose sources; the Stoic philosopher Epictetus did not write poetry. "Appearance" (Greek *phantasia*) is a key word in the moral *Discourses* of Epictetus and the first two lines are clearly a direct translation of the Greek extract given on page 60. Indeed it appears that Stephanides has adapted the eighteenth-century translation of Elizabeth Carter which reads "Appearance, wait for me a little. Let me see what you are, and what you represent" (*Epictetus* (Carter), page 157), adding the word "breath" and omitting the repetition of "what you", thus making two lines in iambic pentameter, and providing a rhyme for "Death" in the third line. In the original context these words are not an apostrophe to the abstract concept of "appearance", but a recommended way of dealing with a "base and sordid" appearance which may lead you astray ("be not hurried along by it . . . but say 'Appearance, wait for me . . .'"). There seems to be no specific passage in Epictetus which could have served as a basis for last two lines of Stephanides' quatrain. The words "give me just time" may be simply a development of "wait for me a little breath", or they may reflect Epictetus' occasional references to the "short time" (*oligos chronos*) of our life. Epictetus sometimes refers to "life" and "death" together, but distinguishing between them is not his chief concern: for him, both are matters of indifference from a moral point of view, since they are not within our power, not subject to our will. "Earth" (*gaia*) and "heavenly things" (*ta ourania*) — Stephanides' "Firmament" — also occasionally occur together in Epictetus, but the emphasis is on their inter-relatedness. This quatrain "after Epictetus" is in fact rather foreign to the mode of Epictetus' thought. The last

line, though, may indicate an awareness of an anonymous epigram "On the 'Manual' of Epictetus" which Paton translates as "Store up in thy heart the counsel of Epictetus, that thou mayest enter into the heavenly recesses, thy soul wafted up from earth to mount to the skies" (*Greek Anthology* III, Book IX, 207).

61. *The astronomer.* Claudius Ptolemaeus is better known simply as Ptolemy, the geographer, astronomer and mathematician — and poet (a polymath like Stephanides) — who lived in Alexandria in the second century AD. The version of this translation published as the first of "Three quatrains" on page 58 of *Cities of the Mind* has a full stop instead of an exclamation mark at the end, but is otherwise identical.

63. *The lover.* In the original, not just a sip, but a whole jug of wine has been drunk, in contrast to a morsel of mealcake; and the "true-love" is named as Poliagre, but she is not said to be *hurrying by*, or indeed present.

63. *The exile.* "Corcyra" is the ancient name of Corfu, Stephanides' home from the age of eleven, when the family left India, to the outbreak of the Second World War; and this perhaps explains the appeal of Julius' epigram. The Greek text actually refers to the island by a different ancient name, "Scheria", the land of the Phaeacians in Homer's *Odyssey*, traditionally identified with Corfu (though not all authorities concur in this).

63. *Epitaph for Leonidas and his Three Hundred.* In the *Typescript* the author is given as "Simonides of Cos". This has been amended to "Simonides of Ceos" to avoid confusion. Ceos (Latin) is the island in the Cyclades now known as Kea, but *Keôs* in Ancient Greek. Cos or Kos (Ancient Greek *Kôs*) is a different island, in the Dodecanese, but it seems that in Antiquity this name was sometimes also used for the Cycladic island of Ceos, and the lyric poet and epigrammatist is indeed still referred by some as "Simonides of Cos". The Greek says "obedient to *their* laws (or commands)", but, given that in this epigram Spartans (Lacedaemonians) are addressing their fellow-Spartans, Stephanides' sub-

stitution of "our" makes sense. Leonidas was the Spartan king who, leading a force of three hundred Spartans (and many other Greeks), held the narrow pass at Thermopylae for several days against a vastly superior Persian army in 480 BC.

65. *Epitaph to the Spartan dead at Plataea.* In both the *Typescript* and *Island Trails* the author is given as "Simonides of Cos": on the substitution of Ceos for Cos, see the previous note. "Yet" at the beginning of the third line is taken from the version in *Island Trails*; the *Typescript* has "But". Plataea was the site of the final battle in the Greek repulse of the second Persian invasion, in 479 BC (the year following the Greek defeat at Thermopylae referred to in the preceding poem).

65. *The hypochondriac's epitaph.* No Greek source has as yet been traced for this poem. Its inclusion here is based on the heading in *Autumn Gleanings* (page 130): "*The hypochondriac's epitaph (after the ancient Greek)*". It is possible that "after the ancient Greek" is a jest, and that no Greek original exists. The punch line, in the form "I told you I was ill", has become well known in recent years as the epitaph which the comedian Spike Milligan (1915– 2002) requested for his own gravestone. (The Diocese of Chichester, however, would only permit it when translated into Irish, and it appears as "Dúirt mé leat go raibh mé breoite".) Contrary to a common assumption, Spike Milligan did not dream up his final joke. In the form "I told you I was sick" it has appeared on many gravestones in the last fifty years, particularly in the USA, as an Internet image search on this phrase will demonstrate. Variants include "*See*, I told you I was sick" and "I told you I was *really* sick" evoking other elements of Stephanides' poem. Spike Milligan was interested in the Classics, and an ultimate source — both for his and other actual epitaphs and for Stephanides' literary epitaph — in some humorous Greek sepulchral epigram cannot yet be ruled out, though it is strange that such a source should prove so elusive. If any reader knows of or can trace a Greek source, please inform the publisher so that it can be included in a later edition.

SOURCES OF THE GREEK TEXTS AND TRANSLATIONS

The short titles of the sources are listed in alphabetical order. The list includes works cited only in the Introduction or Notes.

Autumn Gleanings
Theodore Stephanides. *Autumn Gleanings: Corfu memoirs and poems*. Edited by Richard Pine, Lindsay Parker, James Gifford and Anthony Hirst. Kerkyra: The Durrell School of Corfu; Pine Bluff, AR: The International Lawrence Durrell Society; 2011. Reprinted with minor corrections 2012, 2015. ISBN 978-0-9549937-3-3.

Cities of the Mind
Theodore Stephanides. *Cities of the Mind*. London: The Fortune Press, 1969.

Epictetus (Carter)
The Moral Discourses of Epictetus, translated by Elizabeth Carter, 2nd Dent edition, vol. I. London: J. M. Dent and Co., 1902; first published in 1758 as part of *All the works of Epictetus, which are now extant; consisting of his Discourses, preserved by Arrian in four books, the Enchiridion, and Fragments*.

Epictetus (Schenkl)
Epicteti dissertationes ab Arriani digestae, edited by Henricus Schenkl. Stuttgart: Teubner, 1916 (1st edition 1894).

Greek Anthology I
The Greek Anthology, vol. I. Edited and translated by W. R. Paton, 1st edition. London: William Heinemann; Cambridge, MA: Harvard University Press; 1916.

SOURCES

Greek Anthology II
 The Greek Anthology, vol. II. Edited and translated by W. R. Paton, 1st edition. London: William Heinemann; Cambridge, MA: Harvard University Press; 1917.

Greek Anthology III
 The Greek Anthology, vol. III. Edited and translated by W. R. Paton, 1st edition. London: William Heinemann; Cambridge, MA: Harvard University Press; 1915.

Greek Anthology IV
 The Greek Anthology, vol. IV. Edited and translated by W. R. Paton, 1st edition. London: William Heinemann; Cambridge, MA: Harvard University Press; 1918.

If not, winter
 If not, winter: Fragments of Sappho, translated by Anne Carson. New York: Alfred A. Knopf, 2002. ISBN 0-375-41067-8.

Island Trails
 Theodore Stephanides. *Island Trails*. With an Introduction by Gerald Durrell. London: Macdonald and Company, 1973.

Lyra Graeca I
 Lyra Graeca: Being the remains of all the Greek lyric poets from Eumelus to Timotheus excepting Pindar, vol. I: *Including Terpander Alcman Sappho and Alcaeus*. Edited by J. M. Edmonds, 1st edition. London: William Heinemann; Cambridge, MA: Harvard University Press; 1922.

Lyra Graeca Ia
 Lyra Graeca: Being the remains of all the Greek lyric poets from Eumelus to Timotheus excepting Pindar, vol. I: *Including Terpander Alcman Sappho and Alcaeus*. Edited by J. M. Edmonds, 2nd, revised and enlarged edition. London: William Heinemann; Cambridge, MA: Harvard University Press; 1928.

Lyra Graeca II
: *Lyra Graeca: Being the remains of all the Greek lyric poets from Eumelus to Timotheus excepting Pindar*, vol. II: *Including Stesichorus Ibycus Anacreon and Simonides*. Edited by J. M. Edmonds. London: William Heinemann; Cambridge, MA: Harvard University Press; 1924.

Sappho (Wharton)
: Henry Thornton Wharton. *Sappho: Memoir, Text, Selected Renderings, and Literal Translation*, 4th edition. London: John Lane, 1905.

Sappho and Alcaeus (Page)
: Denys Page. *Sappho and Alcaeus: An Introduction to the Study of Ancient Lesbian Poetry*. Oxford: Clarendon Press, 1955.

Typescript
: Theodore Ph. Stephanides. "Translations of some of the extant poems of Sappho of Lesbos (*circa* 620 B.C.)." Typescript, bound in a card cover, in the British Library, shelfmark YA.1992.b.6109.

Worlds in a Crucible
: Theodore Stephanides. *Worlds in a Crucible*. London: Mitre Press, 1973. ISBN 0-7051-0179-7.

INDEX OF PERSONS AND PLACES

This is an index of persons and places in the ancient world (historical, mythological, astronomical). It includes all the authors of the Greek poems, other than Sappho. References to Sappho are indexed only where they occur within the poems (her own or those of others). It includes all references to places and to persons both in the poems and (except for references to Sappho) in the Introduction (roman numerals) and the Notes (page numbers in the range 67–77).

Achaeans xii, 53, 71, 73, 74
Acheron xii
Achilles 74
Agamemnon xii, 53, 74
Ajax 74
Alcaeus vii, 21, 70
Alexandria 59, 76
Anacreon xiv, 63
Anactoria x–xi, 37, 39, 67, 70, 72–3
Antilochus 74
Antipater of Sidon vii
Aphrodite ix, xii, xvi, 17, 27, 29, 31, 59, 69, 70, 71–2, 73 (*see also* Cypris)
Asia Minor 67
Athenaeus 68
Atreus 51, 74
Atridae/Atreides 51, 74
Atthis ix, xii, 21, 37, 41, 70, 72, 73

Bacchus 74
Brochea/Brocheo x–xi

Ceos 63, 65, 76, 77
Claudius Ptolemaeus 61, 76
Clearchus 68
Cleis viii, x, 9, 15, 67, 68, 72
Corcyra 63, 76

Corfu 76
Corinth 75
Cos 76, 77
Crete 17, 29, 70, 71
Cronus 72
Cyclades 76
Cypris 15, 43, 69, 73 (*see also* Aphrodite)
Cyprus 69
Cythera 69

Demetrius of Phalerum 70
Dica 15, 69 (*see also* Mnesidice)
Dione 72
Dionysus 74
Dodecanese 76

Elysian Fields 74
Epictetus xiv, 61, 75–6
Eros xvi, 13, 27
Eumelus 65
Eurydice 73

Gongyla ix–x, xii, 43, 53, 73, 74
Gorgo ix, 1, 23, 71
Graces, the 15, 69

Helen (of Troy) 23, 39, 71, 72–3
Hera xiii, 51, 74

INDEX OF PERSONS AND PLACES

Hermes xii, 53, 74
Hermione 23, 71
Homer/Homeric xvi, 73, 74, 76
Hyccara 75

Ilium/Ilion 51, 74 (*see also* Troy)

Julius Polyaenus 63

Kea/Keôs 76
Kos/Kôs 76
Klêïs *see* Cleis
Knossos xii, 29, 70, 71

Lacedaemonians 63, 76–7 (*see also* Spartans)
Laïs 59, 75
Leonidas ix, xiv, 65, 76–7
Lesbos/Lesbian vii, 1, 61, 67, 69, 70, 74 (*see also* Mytilene)
Lydia/Lydian 7, 15, 37, 39, 67, 72, 73

Macedonia 68
Malta/Maltese xiv, 65
Maximus of Tyre 67
Menelaus 71, 72–3, 74
Minoans 71
Mnesidice 69 (*see also* Dica)
Muses, the xvi, 1, 7, 9, 45, 61, 67, 69
Mycenae 74
Mytilene xiii, 51, 74 (*see also* Lesbos)

Olympus 68
Orpheus 45, 72–3
Oxyrhynchus x, 68

Palladas 59
Paris 71, 72–3

Patroclus 74
Persephone 15
Persians 77
Phaeacians 76
Phalerum 70
Pierian Spring 13, 68
Pindar 67
Plataea 65, 77
Plato ix, 1, 59, 61
Pleiades ix, 1, 17, 55, 69
Poliagre 76
Ptolemy 76 (*see also* Claudius Ptolemaeus)

Sappho 1, 9, 21, 31, 41, 45, 47, 49, 51, 53, 55, 61
Sardis 37, 63, 72
Scamander (river) 51, 74
Scheria 76
Seven Sisters 70
Sicily 73
Simonides ix, xiv, 63, 65, 76
Socrates 67
Spartans 65, 76–7 (*see also* Lacedaemonians)

Taurus 69
Thermopylae 77
Thyone 51, 74
Timas ix, 15, 69
Troy/Trojan xvi, 39, 51, 701, 72–3, 74 (*see also* Ilium)
Tymnes 65
Tyre 67

Underworld 73
Uranus 72

Xanthippe 67

Zeus xvi, 13, 31, 51, 63, 71–2, 74

GREEK INDEX OF FIRST LINES

Ἄγε δῖα χέλυννά μοι 4
αἰ δ' ἦχες ἔσλων ἴμμερον ἢ κάλων 20
αἰ δέ μοι γάλακτος ἐπάβολ' ἦσκε 48
αἶσ' ἔγων ἔφαν· Ἄγαναι γύναικες 26
ἀλλ' ἄγιτ', ὦ φίλαι 8
ἀλλ' ἔμ' ὀλβίαν ἀδόλως ἔθηκαν 6
ἀμφὶ δ' ὔδωρ / ψῦχρον ὤνεμος κελάδει δι' ὔσδων 18
Ἄσβεστον κλέος οἴδε φίλῃ περὶ πατρίδι θέντες 64
Ἀστέρας πρὶν μὲν ἔλαμπες ἐνὶ ζωοῖσιν Ἔῳος 58
Ἄστερες μὲν ἀμφὶ κάλαν σελάνναν 20
Ἄτθι, σοὶ κἄμ' Ἀνακτορία φίλα 36
Ἀτθιδ' οὔποτ' ἄρ' ὄψομαι 40
Ἀτίετε Μοίσαν βαθυκόλπων κάλα δῶρα, παῖδες 44
Γλύκηα μᾶτερ, οὔ τοι δύναμαι κρέκην τὸν ἴστον 16
Δέδυκε μὲν ἀ σελάννα 16
Δεῦρο δηὖτε, Μοῖσαι, χρύσιον λίποισαι 6
δεῦρύ μ' ἐκ Κρήτας ἐπὶ τόνδε ναῦον 28
Διὸς γὰρ πάϊς ἐστ' ὁ χρύσος 12
ἐγὼ δὲ φίλημ' ἀβροσύναν, καί μοι τὸ λάμπρον 12
Εἰ καί σευ πολύφωνος ἀεὶ πίμπλησιν ἀκούσας 62
ἔκδεξαί με μικρόν, φαντασία 60
ἔλθε, Κύπρι, / χρυσίαισιν ἐν κυλίκεσσιν ἄβραις 14
ἔμοι δ' ὠς ἄνεμος κατάρης δρύσιν ἐμπέτων 4
Ἐννέα τὰς Μούσας φασίν τινες· ὡς ὀλιγώρως 60
Ἐπτάξατέ μοι, παῖδες, ἄκα τὰς μεγάλας ὔπισθα 46
Ἔσπερε πάντα φέρων, ὄσα φαίνολις ἐσκέδασ' αὔως 18
Ἔστι μοι κάλα πάϊς χρυσίοισιν ἀνθέμοισιν 14
Ἦλθες· κεῦ ἐποίησας· ἔγω δέ σε 22
ἦρ ἀ / δῆρα το / Γογγύλα τ' ἔφατ' 52
Ἠράμαν μὲν ἔγω σέθεν, Ἄτθι, πάλαι ποτά 20
Ἠρίστησα μὲν ἰτρίου λεπτοῦ μικρὸν ἀποκλάς 62
Ἡ σοβαρὸν γελάσασα καθ' Ἑλλάδος, ἥ ποτ' ἐραστῶν 58
Ἰόπλοκ' ἄγνα μελλιχόμειδε Σάπφοι 20

κὰτ ἔμον στάλαγμον 8
κατθάνοισα δὲ κείσεαι οὐδέ τινι μναμοσύνα σέθεν 12
Κρῆσσαι νύ ποτ' ὦδ' ἐμμελέως πόδεσσιν 16
μάλα δὴ κεκορημένοις / Γόργως 22
μελλίχιος δ' ἐπ' ἰμμέρτῳ κέχυται προσώπῳ 26
Οἱ μὲν ἱππήων στρότον οἱ δὲ πέσδων 38
οἴαν τὰν ὐάκινθον ἐν ὄρρεσι ποίμενες ἄνδρες 18
Οἶδ' ὅτι θάνατος ἐγὼ καὶ εφάμερος· ἀλλ' ὅταν ἄστρων 60
οἶον τὸ γλυκύμαλον ἐρεύθεται ἄκρῳ ἐπ' ὔσδῳ 16
Ὄλβιε γάμβρε, σοὶ μὲν δὴ γάμος, ὡς ἄραο 26
Ὄνοιρε, μελαίνας τέκος ὦ νύκτος, ὃς ἔγγυς αὔως 32
ὁ πλοῦτος δ' ἄνευ ἀρέτας 12
ὄττα γάρ κ' ἐνάντιον εἰσίδω σε 22
οὐ γὰρ θέμις ἐν μοισοπόλῳ οἰκίᾳ 8
Πλάσιον δή μοι κατ' ὄναρ παρείη 50
πλήρης μὲν ἐφαίνετ' ἀ σέλαννα 6
πόδας δε / ποίκιλος μάσλης ἐπέτεννε 6
Ποικίλλεται μὲν γαῖα πολυστέφανος 8
Ποικιλόθρον' ἀθάνατ' Ἀφρόδιτα 30
πτερύγων δ' ὑπακακχέει / λιγύραν ἀοίδαν 18
Σκηνὴ πᾶς ὁ βίος καὶ παίγνιον· ἢ μάθε παίζειν 58
σοὶ χάριεν μὲν εἶδος / κώππατα μελλιχόχροα 26
σὺ δὲ στεφάνοις, ὦ Δίκα, πέρθεσσ' ἐράταις φόβαισιν 14
τάδε νῦν ἐταίραις 4
ταῖσι δὲ ψαῦκρος μὲν ἔγεντο θῦμος 4
Τὰν ταχίσταν, ὦ κέλομαί σ' ὄνελθε 42
Τῆδε τὸν ἐκ Μελίτης ἀγρὸν κύνα φησὶν ὁ πέτρος 64
Τίμαδος ἅδε κόνις, τὰν δὴ πρὸ γάμοιο θάνοισαν 14
τὸ θναίσκην κάκον· οἱ θέοι γὰρ οὕτω 4
τοῦτο δ' ἴσθι, διπλασίαν 6
Φαίνεταί μοι κῆνος ἴσος θέοισιν 34
χρύσειοι δ' ἐρέβινθοι ἐπ' ἀϊόνων ἐφύοντο 4
ψαύην δ' οὐ δοκίμοιμ' ὀράνω ἔσσα διπάχεα 6
Ὦ ξεῖν' ἄγγειλον Λακεδαιμονίοις ὅτι τῇδε 62

ENGLISH INDEX OF TITLES AND FIRST LINES

All entries relate to the poems of Sappho except where another author's name is given in brackets. Titles are in italics. Titles or first lines beginning with "A" or "The" are listed under A or T, not under the first letter of the second word.

A lifetime blessed by Eros 13
A Morning Star, you gladdened us in life (Plato) 59
A mortal I — but when I trace (Claudius Ptolemaeus) 61
A song I will now sing and, at my voice 5
A sweet apple reddens at the tip of the bough 17

After the marriage ceremony 27
Ah, see the love-sick doves, poor things 5
Alcaeus and Sappho 21
Appearance (Epictetus) 61
Appearance, wait for me a little breath (Epictetus) 61

Beyond all other mortals is he blessed 35
Bluebells 19

Come back to me as swiftly as you can 43
Come, Cypris, and in cups of chiselled gold 15
Complaint 17

Death 5
Death is an evil — thus the gods decide 5
Dream, child of night-time, you who to me creep 33
Dying Sappho to Gongyla 53
Dying Sappho to her daughter Cleis 9

Epitaph 15
Epitaph for Leonidas and his Three Hundred 63
Epitaph to a Maltese watch-dog (Tymnes) 65
Epitaph to the Spartan dead at Plataea (Simonides) 65
Evening 19

Farewell to Atthis 41
Flowers 9
Flowers deck both hill and heath 9

ENGLISH INDEX OF TITLES AND FIRST LINES

From underneath its wings 19
Full gleams the moon; and young girls gaze 7

Gold 13
Gold is the child of Zeus 13
Gorgo 23
Gorgo . . . I am sick of her! 23

Had you desired the good and fair 21
Her girdle's fringe hung to her ankles down 7

I did not ever guess, until one night I tried 7
I, Laïs, who once smiled so proud (Plato) 59
I look upon your face and see 23
I loved you, Atthis, at the time 21
I said, "It will be soon." Gongyla said 53
I said: "O honoured women friends 27
I took (for thus do poets lunch) (Anacreon) 63
If my two breasts could still be tense with milk 49
Immortal Aphrodite, rainbow-throned 31
Invocation 7
It is not seemly, daughter, to make moan 9

Laïs' mirror (Plato) 59
Life (Palladas) 59
Love (in Distichs) 5
Love (in Longer poems) 35
Love-sickness 17

May driving storm-winds bear away my tears 9
May I behold before me in a dream 51
Moonlight 21
Moonrise 7
Morning 9
Mother, I cannot spin nor weave 17
My little daughter, Cleis 15

Night 7
Night prayer 7
No more shall I see Atthis; and in truth 41

O Aphrodite, speed from distant Crete 29

ENGLISH INDEX OF TITLES AND FIRST LINES

O Atthis, our dear Anactoria lives 37
O come, my lyre divine, take wing 5
O Dica, with your dainty hands 15
O Evening, you bring back from everywhere 19
O groom, the wedding-feast is past 27
O Stranger, go tell the Lacedaemonians (Simonides) 63
On Gongyla's departure 43
Our songs must end, companions dear 9

Prayer 9

Retrospect 13

Sappho greets her pupils 47
Sappho in exile 51
Sappho refuses to marry again 49
Sappho to her pupils 45
Sappho's lament to Aphrodite 31
Sepulchral epigram (Plato) 59
See! I was right in spite of all their jeers (Anon.) 65
Setting Pleiades (Stephanides) 55
Some claim the fairest thing on this dark earth 39
Some say / there are Nine Muses (Plato) 61
Such was the reverence and awe inspired (Stephanides) 1
Sweet-eyed Sappho, to you I come 21

The altar 17
The apple 17
The astronomer (Claudius Ptolemaeus) 61
The boor 13
The cicada 19
The departure of Anactoria 37
The doves 5
The exile (Julius Polyaenus) 63
The farewell 27
The garden 19
The girdle 7
The Golden Muses gave me all delight 7
The hypochondriac's epitaph (Anon.) 65
The lover (Anacreon) 63
The lyre 5

ENGLISH INDEX OF TITLES AND FIRST LINES

The moon has set, the Pleiades 17
The oak-tree bends before the headlong wind 5
The Pleiades that Sappho sang (Stephanides) 55
The river 5
The river flows, cold from the mountain snow 5
The return 23
The shepherds lead their flock to grass 19
The snow-white Maltese dog beneath this loam (Tymnes) 65
The song 5
The stars around the lovely Moon 21
The Tenth Muse (Plato) 61
The Tenth Muse (Stephanides) 1

This life's a stage, a jest. Then learn to play (Palladas) 59
Through channel-troughs of apple-wood 19
Through these sweet hours, believe me when I say 7
Thus danced the happy girls of Crete 17
Timas lies here, led on her wedding day 15

To a dream 33
To a friend 23
To Anactoria 39
To Aphrodite of Knossos 29
To Atthis 21
To Dica 15
To her baby daughter Cleis 15
To the Muses 7

Upon their own dear land eternal fame (Simonides) 65

Wealth and virtue 13
Wealth that knows not Virtue 13
Wine 15

You came. And you did well to come 23
You hid yourselves, O children, crouching down 47
You slight the Muses, children, when you say 45
You will be dead forever; aye, no breath 13
Your golden home, O Muses, on this day 7

Zeus, you who rule Corcyra's holy shore (Julius Polyaenus) 63